REVOLUTION: A CHALLENGE OF LOVE is an intense experience, leading the reader to question the most fundamental aspects of our society. The author goes directly to the core of the problem and challenges the establishment and all people through a series of bold and powerful questions that stimulate the reader. As the questions are asked—and answered in the reader's own mind—a new awareness emerges of the need for growth and change to create a world of justice and peace. This profoundly challenging book will change forever the way you look at yourself and the world around you. It will enable you to place in perspective the great questions of our time as well as the most intimate and fundamental day-to-day problems we all encounter. It presents a challenge that every individual in our society can join. It rejects the voice that tells us our opinion and efforts do not matter. It unequivocally tells us that "together we can" make a difference for ourselves and for our children. As you follow this journey of discovery with author Anthony G. Bottagaro, you will find yourself sometimes laughing, sometimes weeping and always greatly moved. **REVOLUTION: A CHALLENGE OF LOVE** will bring you renewed hope, a positive direction for the future and confidence in yourself and those around you. This book opens the windows of our minds and allows a breath of fresh air to blow away the veils of obscurity.

In praise of REVOLUTION: A CHALLENGE OF LOVE

"REVOLUTION raises a succession of compelling and pointed questions which challenge the reader. Didn't they kill Socrates for asking questions?"
—*Richard C. Nehls, Attorney-At-Law*

"Confrontation. A touch of guilt. An indictment of the organized churches."
—*Anonymous Clergyman*

"In REVOLUTION, Tony Bottagaro challenges organized Christianity to now turn and humbly bow its head before the cross and ask forgiveness for neglecting its spiritual mission. He further challenges Christianity to become reborn with the spiritual message of Jesus, 'love one another as I have loved you.'"
—*John D. Hay, Founder, Celestial Seasonings, Inc.*

"Enlightening. Spiritual. Makes the reader really think down deep. Touches everyday reality."
—*Laurie Enderson, College Student*

"REVOLUTION is food for the soul."
—*Patterson Benero, Journalist*

"REVOLUTION penetrates the religious beliefs, ethics and morals of all people. Touches every lifestyle . . ."
—*Jo Ann Hallett, Executive*

REVOLUTION
A Challenge of Love
by Anthony G. Bottagaro

REVOLUTION
A Challenge of Love
by Anthony G. Bottagaro

REVOLUTION: A CHALLENGE OF LOVE

Copyright © 1988 by Anthony G. Bottagaro
All Rights Reserved
This book may not be reproduced in whole or in part, by mimeograph or any other means, without permission.

For information write:
  Interloc Publishing Inc.
  P.O. Box 79
  Boulder, Colorado 80306

Library of Congress Catalog Card Number 88-083222
ISBN 0-9621433-0-8

Printed in the United States of America

I dedicate *REVOLUTION: A CHALLENGE OF LOVE* to my family, my wife Cathy and our children, Kathleen, Andy, Monica, David and Tom and his wife Dina. To my mother, father, mother-in-law and father-in-law, and all my relatives, friends, and all those who consider me an adversary. To all people in our neighborhood, community, county, state, country, continent, and indeed the whole earth who are family, who are in fact all one.

ACKNOWLEDGMENT

I give thanks to the living God our Father, who through the Holy Spirit brings forth the truth and knowledge of the Universe, which is in and through all people.

CONTENTS

INTRODUCTION: The Journey Continues 1
CHAPTER ONE: Declarations of Revolution 7
CHAPTER TWO: Risk 15
CHAPTER THREE: Hierarchy and Leaders 23
CHAPTER FOUR: Hardness of Heart 33
CHAPTER FIVE: Conspiracy of Silence 45
CHAPTER SIX: Man-Made Rules
  and Regulations 57
CHAPTER SEVEN: Hypocrisy 69
CHAPTER EIGHT: Law of Love 79
CHAPTER NINE: Spiritual Bondage 89
CHAPTER TEN: Brick and Mortar 101
CHAPTER ELEVEN: Power of Guilt 111
CHAPTER TWELVE: Word and Deed 121
CHAPTER THIRTEEN: Disunity 131
CHAPTER FOURTEEN: The Mountain
  of Injustice 143
CHAPTER FIFTEEN: To Create a World
  More Human and More Divine 155
CHAPTER SIXTEEN: Together We Can 169

INTRODUCTION

The Journey Continues...

"Go to this nation and say, you will hear and hear again, but not understand, see and see again but not perceive. For the heart of this nation has grown coarse, their ears are dull of hearing and they have shut their eyes, for fear they should see with their eyes, hear with their ears, understand with their heart, and be converted and healed by me." Isaiah 6:9-10

The book REVOLUTION: A CHALLENGE OF LOVE is a challenge to all people to create a world more human and more divine with a revolution of truth through the heart and mind.

I dare to dream that this vision can be achieved because it requires no money, special classes, or books; we need only to live life to the fullest and love one another.

I write this book *REVOLUTION: A CHALLENGE OF LOVE* as a Christian, realizing that many of its readers will come from different religious perspectives. I ask for your patience as I will attempt to bring forward the challenge of revolution in truth, using Jesus Christ as the living example. I do so with the hope of not offending anyone who is not a Christian, but contrary to that, it is because of my personal relationship with him, Jesus Christ, that I have been allowed to live, see, hear and understand with my heart, unity in diversity. I ask you to stay with revolution until the end, to give me a chance to tell it the way I see it. You may see it differently and that's all right, for we serve the same God, our Father. I believe the strength and power to change this world is with us, all the people who comprise all religions and nations and sustain society.

I believe our ability to reach unity in diversity will accomplish the goal of creating a society inspired by God through love. Together, we are one in this ongoing and challenging adventure in our search for freedom, justice and peace.

Our God is a living God, a Father who gives us his love without condition. All he asks in return is for us to love one another without condition.

There is a new wind blowing that is full of light, energy and life, and the success of this endeavor depends on our love and the power of God that comes with it. We need to challenge all people to allow their lives to be guided by love and faith, thereby creating a fusion of the heart and mind within themselves and throughout society.

In 1983 I wrote the message *TO CREATE A WORLD MORE HUMAN AND MORE DIVINE*, which is included in this book. Through this message, I have been actively involved with the leadership in the religious, social, business and political realms. After many years of involvement, I have repeatedly seen the discrepancy between word and deed in the conduct of some of the leadership on this earth. More often than not, they use a one-track solution to problems that are entrenched in the institutionalized intellect. I am afraid at times that the hierarchy of some governments and religious as well as secular institutions and organizations, have become insensitive to life, and are caught up in the maze and entanglement of their structures. Therefore, instead of a foundation of love, we find one of hypocrisy and hardness of heart.

Until the leadership can lead with total wholeness, with a fusion of the heart and mind in the decision-making process, we will continue to stay in place, just stirring up dust rather than moving forward.

Part of the problem is that every now and then, we the people, are fed a distorted picture and are unaware of the seriousness and long-term effect of a particular concern or issue. This problem must be remedied if we, as a people, are to be effective. Everyone of us is a dominant force here on earth, and by our actions, we impact each segment of our lives and the lives of others. However, what paralyzes life, is a lack of faith and a lack of courage. I, for one, am not content with misery or mediocrity.

I refuse to believe that we cannot change this world into a world more human and more divine. I cannot help but wonder what would become of humanity if all the people of all nations accepted the freedom that the living God our Father gives us through the

Spirit. The Holy Spirit that is implanted in us gives life and frees the heart to live in light and truth.

We, as individuals, have great human resources. Our resources in life include the gifts of faith, enthusiasm, patience, wisdom, strength, understanding, trustfulness, imagination, self control, forgiveness, humility, hope, energy, courage, gentleness, kindness, joy, and love. When we share these resources with each other, out of love, in whatever we are and whatever we do, the residual effect we have on society will be lasting. Then, people will begin to recognize the Kingdom of God, which is now; it is in us, and among us.

I believe the time has come to challenge all people, especially those in a position of influence, whether in the religious or secular realm, back to the basic law of love, because God is love. There can be no dichotomy between the spiritual and the intellect, as the living God our Father is the reality embracing all reality. When we acknowledge and accept the spiritual and intellectual fusion of the heart, mind and soul, we can cut through the illusion of worldly matters and recognize each other, for we are one. Then all of our daily actions will find purpose and meaning as we move forward toward our destiny.

The prophet tried to reform the religious, social and political life of his people. He taught that the heart of religion is an individual's personal relationship with God and emphasized the importance of the individual. My vision is that of the prophet, as his spirit still lives.

The cornerstone of revolution is Jesus Christ and the internal weave of personal transformation which is based on love. The spirit of Christ is letting it be known that once again it is time to tear up and knock down, to build up and to plant. In order to create a world more human and more divine, we cannot fail in our responsibility to God, or to humankind, for we are linked together as one.

It is my prayer that *REVOLUTION: A CHALLENGE OF LOVE* can fulfill the vision.

CHAPTER 1

Declarations of Revolution

To: All religious and secular institutions and organizations and all people.

I ask and challenge you to a revolution of love. I challenge you to think about, and act on, the declarations of revolution, and answer in your heart and mind, the questions that pertain to them.

I will not give up or fade away, and I refuse to believe that we cannot change this world. I invite you to join me in a revolution of truth, in order to bring this world together in peace and joy through love. Our success in this endeavor will be determined by our love and the depth of our belief and faith in the living God, our Father. The time to act is now.

If you care about life and if you care about truth, accept this challenge. Together we can.

Sincerely,

Tony Bottagaro

Tony Bottagaro

Declarations of Revolution

I declare a revolution to overthrow the following powers of darkness and to rebuild them with the commandment of love and the living God as cornerstone, through a fusion of the heart and mind. I declare a revolution to overthrow and rebuild all or any part of any religious and secular institutions, philosophies and organizations*...

ONE... where the hierarchy and other leaders in the religious and secular realms seek to be served rather than serve and do not hear, see, or understand the people, instilling want, fear and slavery in the hearts and minds of all people.

TWO... where the development of hardness of heart now obscures and suffocates the people's dignity and endowed abilities to change society and keeps peace an impossible dream for all people.

*See page 12

THREE . . . where there exists a conspiracy of silence that originates and perpetuates a contempt for basic human rights, resulting in degrading treatment of, and crimes against, all people.

FOUR . . . where man-made religious rules and regulations, instituted by cowardice, create fear and distort and eliminate growth in the Spirit of Truth in all people.

FIVE . . . where hypocrisy permeates, confuses, deforms and smothers the spirit of brotherhood and sisterhood toward one another and clouds the real meaning of life and the destiny of all people.

SIX . . . which rather than living the law of love, exploit humankind by butchering fundamental freedoms for their own self-gain, resulting in all forms of tyranny and injustice to all people.

SEVEN . . . that have enforced by doctrine, arrogance and power, spiritual bondage which affects all people by blinding them to truth and obstructing unity and their personal freedom to continue their return back home to the living God, Father of all people.

EIGHT . . . where the brick and mortar and other building materials of churches, mosques, temples and other places of worship are for the sake of structure only, using a cornerstone of materialism and/or bankrupt religious spirit which is fruitless and worthless and produces nothing for all people.

NINE . . . which perpetuate themselves through the power of guilt, greed, false teaching and secrecy, causing resentment, anger and paranoia, which corrode like gangrene in all people.

TEN . . . which employ and accept the discrepancy between word and deed and the crippling of the spirit of life for self-preservation, causing frustration, mistrust and hate in all people.

ELEVEN . . . that cause disunity among people and discriminate either in race, color, sex, religion, or national origin, generating turmoil and barbarous acts at the expense of all people.

TWELVE . . . which harbor aggression, injustice, conceit, fanaticism, discrimination, ignorance, manipulation, ruthlessness, repression, contempt, imprudence, apathy, paranoia, rejection, hostility, cynicism, revenge, pride, savagery, lying, arrogance, misrepresentation, lethargy, blasphemy, affliction, hate, slaughter, cheating, endless disputes, anxiety, anger, deceit, resentment, condemnation, prejudice, self-pity, exploitation, hypocrisy, rivalry, distortion, bigotry, violence, slander, spiritual pride, oppression, sorcery, perjury, disharmony, corruption, suspicion, vengefulness, wrangling, torture, callousness, idolatry, jealousy, radicalism, irresponsibility, pig-headedness, intimidation, hardness of heart, slavery, obstinacy, narrowness, self-centeredness, recklessness, greed, fear, tyranny, rudeness, bribery, indecency, ungratefulness, wickedness, irritation, stubbornness, intolerance, trickery, falsehood, malice, envy, madness, secrecy, militantness, cruelness, feuds, treachery, bitterness, mercilessness, irrationality, spite, mistrust, threats, dishonesty, antagonism, cowardice, defeat, neglect, disillusionment, underhandedness, libel, mindless zealotry, spiritual bondage and any other evil outrage against all people.

If these declarations are true, nothing will stop the revolution. You decide if they are true or not. If they are not true, condemn them. If they are true, meet the challenge of love, and join the revolution.

---

*Religious organizations and institutions include but are not limited to the following: Christian denominations that include Baptists, Church of Christ, Episcopalians, Lutherans, Methodists, Mormons, Orthodox, Pentecostal, Presbyterians, Roman Catholics, United Church of Christ, Seventh Day Adventists, Churches of God, Church of the Nazarene, Eastern Orthodox Churches, Evangelical, Independent Fundamental Churches, Congregational Churches, Jehovah's Witnesses, Mennonite, Reformed Churches, Society Of Friends, Unitarian Universalist; Judaism; Islam; Zoroastrianism; Shinto; Taoism; Confucianism; Hinduism; Sikhism; Jainism; Bahä í Faith; Buddhism; New Age philosophies; Church of Religious Science; Church of Scientology; Unity Church; Unification Church; Hare Krishna; and all other sects and cults. Secular organizations and institutions include but are not limited to the following: arts, business, charities, economics, education, energy, entertainment, environment, government, health and medicine, labor, media, military, nations, politics, research and space, science and technology, social services, sports and transportation.

Tony Bottagaro

Acknowledgment

CHAPTER 2

Risk

I have thought long and hard about whether to include some of my experiences and reactions on the journey to create a world more human and more divine in the book *REVOLUTION: A CHALLENGE OF LOVE*. I have decided to do so for two reasons. First, we all share in what I do, for all my actions, reactions, setbacks and achievements are in Christ. What is true and takes place for me also relates to you. The absolute fact is that we all affect one another. Second, I felt that this was an important ingredient to include in this book, so you would not think I am an arm-chair general, philosopher or theologian. I am in fact a foot-soldier, an ordinary person, who is writing to you through my experiences rather than through some abstract method. I tell you this not for self-praise, but to share with you my roller-coaster ride in life. In this ride, the message of Christ, which is rooted in love, guides me as I attempt to fuse the heart and mind.

I can sense my limitations, as I strive to overcome failure, sickness, rejection, apathy or loneliness. Further, I am also aware of the ego trip that could result from favor or acceptance. However, I do not take myself so seriously that I do not have time to laugh, for I know how important it is to laugh. Without the spiritual weave of Jesus Christ in my body, I would have been crushed. I know without any doubts my interdependence with the living God, my Father, and all his people, as I live life. With that knowledge, I gain my strength to move forward.

In this life journey, I have heard of, observed, committed and been affected by the violations that are described in the declarations. I will not cite specifics, such as people, places and instances. They, who read or hear of the declarations of revolution, will know of whom I speak. I reject naming "names" because to do so will look like an attack on certain persons, rather than their actions. In all cases it is the action to which I am bringing attention. How can I, or anyone else, attack any person? If we are one, wouldn't I then be attacking myself? In all my interactions with people, I try not to see them as different, for I know we are one.

Before 1981, life was nothing more to me than living on this earthly plane with the accepted practices for living. The achievements and goals of having a wife and children, job, home and other material things meant so much to me. I wanted to live the "life" rules and regulations of both the secular and religious world. At that time, religion to me was a place to go to, with its rules and regulations, separate and distinct from life.

In January of 1981, for whatever reason, Christ,

who I now know is in all of us all the time anyway, decided to make his presence felt in an overwhelming way. He found me when I wasn't looking. I immediately began to seek the truth and embark upon a journey to serve him, the Living God, our Father.

Since that time, I have been learning, growing, laughing, crying, experiencing, interacting, praying and relating to Jesus Christ, my Lord and Savior, and his people. In this process, I have had the opportunity to take a retreat every year, consisting of one week alone, seeking the will of our heavenly Father. Out of those retreats have come a deeper understanding of my call and direction in life's journey.

In 1983, prayer, retreats and friends, shaped the message *TO CREATE A WORLD MORE HUMAN AND MORE DIVINE*. The message, a fervent appeal to all, is to create a society inspired by God through love. The message speaks of peace by establishing unity in diversity through Jesus Christ and the subtle power of love. In 1984, a documentary film of the same title was produced. The film premiered at the Dag Hammarskjold Auditorium at the United Nations, and both the book and film were awarded the prestigious Angel Award from Excellence in Media. The book and film were both launched without promotion or publicity, and continue to find their way throughout society.

The simplicity of the message confronts the paranoia, legalism and competition that exist within institutions, both religious and secular. The message and I have been and continue to be supported, rejected and met with apathy in religious circles. I have found that the secular community greets the message with more openness. However, in both the religious and secular realms, the higher up the hierarchical ladder you climb, the more protective and convoluted are the reactions to the call of the message. I give thanks for those courageous people and especially for those in leadership who have strong hearts and are willing to risk their futures for others.

I work for Christ because I love him, and I have taken his message to the people without involvement in any organization. In my opinion, an organization would have suffered from the arrows of competition, and the message may have been buried in a sea of muck. My role and vision here on earth is not just to recite the words within the message, but to take an active part in worldly affairs, whenever and wherever I can.

Speaking from my own experiences, it is not easy for me to recall truth every second of every minute of every day. I realize my own limitations and humanness. Each moment, each day, brings a new experience from which to learn and grow. I try to live a balanced life, and at times I begin to question whether or not I'm a coward. When that thought process begins to take hold, that is the time I try to reach deep into my soul for courage. It is then that I realize that the grace of God is all I need, and the gift of courage is part of that grace.

We are all faced with many diversions and temptations that are so easy to fall prey to. I have had numerous failings, consciously and unconsciously, in my attempt to live out truth. In this quest, I know I have tested the inexhaustible patience of God. But fortunately our God is a loving Father who is all forgiving and continues to give his courage and strength to break the illusion of earth in order to move forward towards our destiny. Out of that comes a strong desire to perfect the relationship with the divine within, the Christ within. When I am in tune with why I am on earth, life becomes more challenging, satisfying and joyful. However, I do not fool myself, for the roadway is still long and rocky on the way back home. In my opinion, the only way to smooth it is to die daily to self so that it is no longer we that live, but that it is Christ that lives in us.

There is not any way to test love without plunging it into society. I have had, and continue to have, my share of problems. I learn from trying to solve these problems by trial and error. I have strived to live my life as an indivisible whole. I am an ordinary person, full of faults, doing whatever I can do to the best of my abilities. I am fully aware of the need for interdependence with each other as we labor on our journey to fulfill our destiny. In this journey, I have had the opportunity to experience much joy and sorrow, negative and positive energy and to choose between love and hate. I have had many wonderful experiences of joy and excitement working with a variety of people and leaders as together we try to build a better society. I had the opportunity to experience a financial disaster, a severe illness and other personal setbacks, all in the midst of trying to stay true to the call, to live truth. It was through that pain, that the love of Christ supported me and my wife and our five children. From there I received the courage and realized that the time had come to take the message deeper into all segments of society. I then decided to accelerate my risk in challenging all people, especially those in leadership, to accept their responsibility and allow their lives to be guided by love and faith. I know I may burn some bridges in the process, but if that's what it takes to move forward, then that's what it takes. I am still involved in business and the mainstream of society with the same up's and down's. But I can tell you that I enjoy my ride on destiny. When we are guided by love and faith, we can eliminate the fragmentation between the spiritual and the intellect, thereby creating a society inspired by God through love.

Incidentally, there really is no perfect way to separate the declarations of revolution and the questions that pertain to them. All the declarations are interwoven, and there is no priority, so one can actually domino the other. If we are to be successful in creating a better world, we need to be successful in all the declarations.

The questions in revolution, are questions I hold in my heart and mind, raised from my own experiences and the experiences of others. They are not intended to act as problem finders, but rather to raise the hope and conscience of all people, for the answers and solutions are within all of us. You might find it helpful, if at first, you read revolution in its entirety, and then go back and re-read and reflect deeper on any declarations and/or questions you choose, in any order. This is not a text book or a test, but a call to revolution, therefore you may find questions in areas that may not seem applicable. However, you cannot separate structured society or the people in revolution, for we are all one.

The message TO CREATE A WORLD MORE HUMAN AND MORE DIVINE is my approach to acting on and answering the questions and finding the solutions raised in the declarations of revolution. I hope it can assist you in your response and action to meeting the challenge of love and answering the call to join the REVOLUTION: A CHALLENGE OF LOVE.

CHAPTER 3
Hierarchy and Leaders

I declare a Revolution to overthrow the following powers of darkness and to rebuild them with the commandment of love and the living God as cornerstone, through a fusion of the heart and mind. I declare a Revolution to overthrow and rebuild all or any part of any religious and secular institutions, philosophies and organizations *where the hierarchy and other leaders in the religious and secular realms seek to be served rather than serve and do not hear, see or understand the people, instilling want, fear and slavery in the hearts and minds of all people.*

I, FOR ONE, ASK:

Why, when some hierarchy and leaders reach a certain level of prestige and acceptability, do they act out of pride and arrogance? Why do they talk about "worldly things" yet flaunt "pomp and circumstance"?

Isn't it true that to lead and be great among the people we must be the servant of all people? Why, when we are the servants, do we look so much to be served?

Why, more often than not, do we take things for granted, and rather than expressing gratitude, we show ingratitude?

Have we pursued vanity so we are now vanity?

Why do some leaders and members of institutions keep themselves busy seeking the bubble reputation that will feed the ego rather than the people?

Why do we look for approval from one another, rather than the approval that comes from God?

Do we base our justification in life by our position in life?

Do the leaders get intoxicated by power?

Why are some of our leaders in government and business afraid to remind their people of their responsibility to God our Father?

Hierarchy and Leaders

Is it true that some in organized religion like to attract attention in their dress and enjoy their title with excessive pride?

Did Jesus Christ have a note-pad, "From the desk of Jesus Christ"?

Why can't we understand that what is given, is given from above?

Is it possible that we can put human glory before God's glory?

If we achieve a greater status in society, does that mean that our responsibility should be greater?

Is respect the one thing in life that we cherish most?

Why do we pride ourselves on spiritual pride?

Is there a game of competition among the organized religions to reach the kingdom of God?

Do we spend our lifetime on earth with the subtlety of threat over our heads? Are we now to the point where we accept threat and fear? Do we believe that sanity is insanity?

How many people are enough to change society to a world inspired by God through love?

If we and society are slow to forgive, how does that impact our relationship with God the Father?

What and where does the law of revenge get us besides an illness that is hidden deep inside?

Are the noble virtues of sincerity and conscientiousness enough, or do they need to be wed to love in order to affect change?

Do we acquire things such as material items and knowledge for the sake of acquisition? Why?

Why is it difficult to learn how to live together as a people? Is it us, or is it them? Who is them?

Can we feel and recognize the presence of evil in society? Can we recognize it by its fruits?

Don't we think that it is about time to disturb the power structure that sits and watches and does nothing?

Doesn't God give us the power to face all adversity?

Hierarchy and Leaders

Have we realized that our highest loyalty is to God our Father?

Why is love approached with apathy?

Have we ever really reflected on the power of the people? Can't an aroused public cause our religious and secular leaders to listen? If the people speak out against injustice, how can the leaders sit by and do nothing?

What is worse, living on a high or low, or living in the gray area of complacency?

Do we place so many demands on ourselves that we end up with the prize of emotional depression? Is depression the result of our constant quest to find happiness in worldly success?

Is it in vogue to compete by undercutting our neighbor?

When failure hits us, do we look inside, or do we lash out against others? Where does our responsibility begin and end?

Do we at times go against our "gut feelings" or intuition? If we do, is it peer pressure in one form or another that pushes us?

Isn't it about time to stand up and make a commitment to life?

Is it easy to criticize so that we can shift the blame onto others? If we do that, then isn't it easy to look to them for the solutions?

Isn't it true that no one can rule another without resentment?

Are we so set in our ways, that to adjust is devastating?

Do we judge ourselves against the feats of others?

Do popularity and success stand in the way of our true destiny?

Who is running our lives? Who is in charge? Is it us, or is it outside influences? Are we puppets? For whom?

Have we invented an institutionalized monster that allows the leaders to control the people? Isn't it wrong for any nation, church or organization to control its people?

Does corruption breed corruption?

Hierarchy and Leaders

Have we even scratched the surface when it comes to the potential of our hearts?

Are we embarrassed if we speak and act with sentiment, compassion, humility and love?

Where is the quest for superiority leading us?

In the act of communicating, doesn't listening play an important part? Do we have a listening heart?

Are the nations in an insane foot race for superiority, built on fear, want, hatred and injustice? Why can't we insist on peace? If we do insist, can any government ignore it?

How much wisdom governs the world?

Have we placed a limit on our own expectations?

Have we taken stock in the words, "this too shall pass"?

Do we run our nations, factories, businesses and religions with fear? Do we always recognize fear and the negative effects it has on us?

Can we stop long enough to recognize one another?

How many times have we been stopped from internal or external progress by an assault of discouragement?

Are we so content with privilege that we grow fat and lazy?

Aren't we challenged by God to accept our responsibility to imitate Christ and love?

Doesn't joy come forth from trials? Isn't the key love? No matter what, love?

Why do we exploit the weak? Don't the weak include people, communities and nations? Don't we realize that we, in turn, exploit ourselves? Isn't the opposite also true? If we gain, everyone gains?

If we have been gifted with leadership, don't we have a major responsibility to all the people?

Do we give to society in order to gain human admiration?

Should we be envious because God our Father is generous? Isn't he generous to all people, no matter their race, color, nationality or rank in society?

Hierarchy and Leaders

Is it true that "the last will be first and the first last"? Doesn't that give us cause to be watchful of our actions all the time, and not be lulled to sleep?

Are we afraid to think for ourselves, to carve out our own path and make a difference?

Do we behave like spoiled children? Aren't the leaders of some institutions like immature children, fighting to be king of the mountain?

Is there such a thing as intellectual snobbery in the institutionalized church? Do our leaders speak to us in a condescending manner? Why is abuse paramount in authority? Doesn't it disgust us?

Isn't it true that Jesus came not to be served, but to serve?

Are the religious leaders caught in a struggle for recognition and promotion?

How in the world can religious leaders call each other phony? Are some so deaf and blind that they have become obstinate or thoughtless?

Do we read our own press-clippings and then congratulate ourselves? Have we become filled with our own self-importance?

WE each need to acknowledge the hierarchy and our leaders, whoever they are, and to take responsibility for their effect on us. The road to self-esteem begins with the first step of accepting ourselves the way we are, and not from worrying about what others say, think or act. Our responsibility is always the same, to love and serve God our Father and all his people. Through love, we can overcome any negativity that we may feel the leadership has inflicted on us.

CHAPTER 4
Hardness of Heart

I declare a Revolution to overthrow the following powers of darkness and to rebuild them with the commandment of love and the living God as cornerstone, through a fusion of the heart and mind. I declare a Revolution to overthrow and rebuild all or any part of any religious and secular institutions, philosophies and organizations *where the development of hardness of heart now obscures and suffocates the people's dignity and endowed abilities to change society and keeps peace an impossible dream for all people.*

I, FOR ONE, ASK:

Why are we concerned with the other person's inequities before we are concerned with our own? Shouldn't we be compassionate as God our Father is compassionate?

Are we, as a people, never satisfied, each going our own way, each after our own interest?

Is it true that the way in which we conduct ourselves is important to the rest of society? How do we rate our conduct with ourselves and others? Do we treat those in our family different than those on the outside? Doesn't the family consist of everyone?

Does ignorance permit cruelty or heartlessness? Is it the ultimate excuse to commit havoc?

Why do we say "peace, peace," yet we act differently? Why don't we believe that peace is possible? Is it because we are caught in the web of negative thinking?

Does a hard heart corrode like gangrene?

Why do we, as a people, keep searching and searching for the ultimate utopia? If we came upon it, would we know it? Is utopia already living in and among us?

Isn't it true that what God wants is love, not sacrifice for the sake of sacrifice?

Do we know God only with our lips, while our hearts are far away?

Hardness of Heart

Is it boastful and arrogant to keep up the outward appearance of religion and to reject the inner power of it?

Isn't it true that a heart of stone can be melted with the power and energy of love?

What can these words, a gift of Christ mean, "peace I give to you, my own peace I give to you, a peace which the world cannot give"?

What will it take to move us in the direction of love and unity? Does it take disaster, tragedy, sickness, hunger or can we break the tradition of despair and reach out to love in hope? Can despair be turned into hope?

Do we believe we are capable of wronging one another? How can we trust and love one another?

Isn't it true that the dignity of people must be preserved? Have our hearts become hard, so that we are dead to the call of help from our brothers and sisters? Have we not accepted the love of God? Have we refused and rejected the love of self?

Is sacrifice joy? Does love take or give?

Will an open heart, like children full of enthusiasm and imagination, change our society for the better?

Why do we always look for secrets and hidden motives in what people do? Who in the world gave birth to paranoia?

Isn't it true that if we recognize Christ we will recognize each other, and therein is unity in diversity? Isn't that a unity so intertwined that it will transcend nations and people of all colors, sexes and classes?

Don't we need to accept our human responsibility out of love and not fear? Will we ask ourselves, "Why didn't I speak out? Why didn't I get involved? Why didn't I care?" Why not defeat defeat with love?

Shouldn't we follow through on our promises and commitments to one another? Aren't broken promises and commitments the basic root of upheaval? Isn't it a root that spreads like wildfire?

Is the question, "why do people have to suffer so much?" or "why does God have to suffer so much?"

If we don't agree with one another, shouldn't we at least love one another?

Hardness of Heart

When we live life, do we live it for ourselves or for all people? Isn't it impossible to live just for ourselves unless we do so out of greed? Does greed justify? If we live life for all people, then won't we find happiness?

Do we think that the Spirit protects us from pain and agony? Or does the Spirit ease the pain and agony and make our burden lighter?

Have we asked ourselves the question, "if I don't stop to help this person in his or her time of need, what will happen?"

Before we go to anyone's aid, do we first weigh the consequences? Do the potential consequences inspire us or restrain us? Do we play it safe for the sake of convenience sake?

Why not accept the challenge to risk living with a fusion of the heart and mind through faith hope and love? Or have words like faith, hope and love become just that, words?

Isn't forgiveness the one practical approach to life? Isn't forgiveness the road to friendship with our adversaries?

How can anyone do anything alone? Do we realize how much we need each other? Are we blind to our interdependence with each other? Do we come to realize that nothing happens to anyone that doesn't affect all of us? And if it affects us, doesn't it affect God?

Is it too radical to inject the concept of love into the classroom? If we do, will it upset the system? Is the system so entrenched in structure that to act on a concept of love would make it look human? If we teach war, conflict and conquest in the classroom, doesn't it seem ludicrous that we do not or cannot teach love?

Is it true that scientists and those in the technological arena burn the midnight oil searching for reality? Isn't reality in us and among us? Isn't reality the living God our Father?

If we are really determined in our quest for peace, shouldn't the walls of injustice come tumbling down? Isn't it then a good idea to keep our focus and our patience on the vision?

If life carries risk anyway, shouldn't we then risk to be happy? Do we get more joy out of being sad and miserable?

If we are constantly fed negative thoughts, aren't we constantly fed a slow death?

Hardness of Heart

When we do the will of the father, isn't it then that our burdens are light? Doesn't that mean we first have to find his will? Doesn't that mean that an open mind and heart will allow us to hear the inner voice?

Why walk in darkness when we could walk in light?

Have we come to the realization that a person alone is incapable? Have we come to the realization that we can change society only with the help of God? How much longer will we wait before we utilize this truth that is in society?

If life is made up of problems, why not take them one at a time and grow in the process? Doesn't life offer endless opportunities? Do we need to rearrange our thought patterns to look to the positive side of life?

Aren't we tired of war, no matter where it takes place? Do we only react when it is close to home? Isn't home the earth? How can we turn our backs?

Can we analyze our situation without God's perspective? Isn't it true that we can see through the eyes of God? Does God see as people see? Don't people look at the illusions of society? Doesn't God look at the heart?

Are we willing to be inconvenienced for what's worthwhile? Is what's worthwhile, the earth, and the people that live there? What joy can we possibly receive from degrading another person? If we diminish others, don't we diminish ourselves?

Isn't it true that when we give our hearts, minds and souls to Christ, all that we are destined to accomplish will come to fruition? Is it then that we can live out life in harmony with the Father and Son?

Isn't love the key to open our eyes and ears and understanding?

Hasn't it been proven that the love of self and others is our defense and offense?

Are we dead to life? Isn't it true that Christ can actually resurrect us from the doldrums of death in mind, heart and spirit? Isn't it true that with Christ, death is nothing more than life, the gateway to our destiny? If Jesus Christ is the resurrection, doesn't he call those who have died and those who live, so that neither will ever see death?

If we have a "give up" attitude, do we close our eyes to injustice? Doesn't that attitude fuel the flame?

Aren't we ourselves the main obstacle to peace? If we have inner peace, will world peace then follow?

If we believe in the power of Christ, why are we astonished when we see success in that power?

How can there be the dignity of people without the power and recognition of the God within all of us?

How could we have let a purge of prayer in the educational system survive? Who could be against love?

Do we have a tendency to look past our success with a doom and gloom attitude? Do we give ourselves enough credit and confidence? Haven't our achievements in the science, space and health fields been amazing? But what about us? Do our achievements in life lead us towards the light? Are we heading in the right direction, or have we become side-tracked and distracted in the illusion? Or are we just quitters?

Should we allow ourselves to be overcome by evil, or should we overcome evil with good?

There are atheists, but so what? Are they immune from love?

Isn't it all right to risk because to love God is to risk? Isn't that our faith? Why not risk in faith if God is within us? Isn't it then, that we turn and depend on him? Didn't he say "fear not"? Doesn't he protect us?

Hasn't God accepted us without any parameters? Doesn't God love us without any condition? Isn't God willing to help us in our journey?

Why do we allow our dignity to be dragged in the mud?

Does worry solve anything? Does worry add anything? If we believe in an all-powerful God the Father, why worry? Is it because it's human to worry?

If we continue to ignore the warning signs, are we on the brink of self-destruction?

When Christ told us to love our enemies, was he being an impractical idealist? Who cares if we are called impractical idealists? Isn't love where the people are?

Where are the slaughterhouses on this planet? Are they both animal and human? Why do we allow them to exist?

Do we use love as a ploy and then start to manipulate with mind control and brainwashing?

Didn't Christ die for us while we were still sinners? Isn't that what forgiveness is all about?

Isn't God always faithful because he cannot disown his own self?

Aren't we always at some critical crossroad?

THE story of love, the unconditional love of God the Father for us and the need for each of us to love one another, needs to be told over and over again until it permeates our entire being. The power of love can remove the veil of complexity from all the systems and energize people as we all strive for a world free of injustice. We can have a new zest for living that is untiring and full of excitement. I believe we need to eat, sleep and breathe love, a love so strong that we will radiate forth a light so powerful, that it will be capable of melting the hardest of hearts. A light that removes the dark forever.

CHAPTER 5
Conspiracy of Silence

I declare a Revolution to overthrow the following powers of darkness and to rebuild them with the commandment of love and the living God as cornerstone, through a fusion of the heart and mind. I declare a Revolution to overthrow and rebuild all or any part of any religious and secular institutions, philosophies and organizations *where there exists a conspiracy of silence that originates and perpetuates a contempt for basic human rights, resulting in degrading treatment of, and crimes against, all people.*

I, FOR ONE, ASK:

Is it true that nations that have skeletons in their own closets are most reluctant to speak out against injustice for fear of retaliation or exposure? Why don't we let the skeletons out of the closet once and for all, forgive and forget and move forward?

At times, don't we, as individuals, keep silent for fear of loss of friendship, rejection, promotion and other actions that can affect us personally?

Isn't it a fact that there exists a conspiracy of silence among people and leadership? Isn't it true that with that conspiracy comes a disregard and contempt for "human rights"? Doesn't it cause us to brutalize each other in the race for power, resulting in crimes against humanity?

Isn't it true that where the conspiracy of silence exists, there is also a lack of hope that feeds on despair and is blind to injustice, which affects every aspect of our life from cradle to grave?

Why maintain the status quo? Are we obedient to public opinion?

Why are we content with lack, limitation, disease, loneliness and failure? Where has hope gone?

Are the rights of all people really protected? Do we admire unlawfulness?

Do we enjoy sitting on the sidelines, judging what is wrong and what is right in society? Do we shift our responsibility to others? Isn't it true that we need to leave the safety of family and the comfort of those around us and be to others what we are to ourselves?

Why is there arrogance among the nations? Why the futile plots against the people? Isn't it true that in some nations, integrity once lived but now there are assassins?

I wonder what the response of God our Father is to the legislation of infamous laws, to those who issue tyrannical decrees and to those who refuse justice to the unfortunate and cheat the poor?

Isn't the gift of peace that God our Father gives us, a peace that the world cannot give? Is it a peace to avoid or escape the world, or a peace of conquest over the darkness? If we accept his peace, won't our wounds be quickly healed?

Shouldn't we search for justice and help the oppressed? Do we vacillate? Do we think we are not worthy? Are we guilt-ridden? Have we condemned ourselves? If we stop and think about the gift of life, how can we not act?

Why, when confronted, are we so willing to be deaf, dumb and blind? Do we come to a halt if confronted with criticism or apathy?

Can it be that the world hates a message of love?

Shouldn't we struggle for what's right? Is it possible to always be tolerant and fair-minded?

Is violence self-perpetuating?

Do we come to a halt if confronted with criticism or apathy?

When we say "nations," aren't we really saying "people"? When we say people, aren't we really saying you and me?

Do we feel more comfortable supporting a cause if it is supported by a number of people? Why should we seek comfort in numbers?

Are we loyal to the institution or organization to the point where we compromise our values and convictions?

Do we depend on society, or does society depend on us?

Why is it that some nations, religions and organizations want to profit at the expense and destruction of others?

Do we really need to understand the viewpoint of our opponents?

If we had Christ's courage, couldn't we fight the "system" and stir up the dust? Isn't it true that we cannot be fair-weather followers?

Shouldn't we share the burdens, and understand the wants and difficulties, of others?

Doesn't peace begin with reconciliation? Aren't we all responsible for the common good of humankind? Why not get involved, and together carry the message of love from the people to all leaders, wherever and whatever their involvement in the systems?

Have the hearts of the nations grown coarse?

Why don't we speak out if we see wrong? What fear or gain keeps us quiet? Why?

Why is there always a movement to shift power?

Haven't the daily acts of violence in our homes, communities and nations outraged the conscience of humankind and prevented a world in which all people can enjoy freedom of speech and belief and freedom from want and fear?

Is it hearing the truth that makes us angry?

Is it true that sometimes we need to burn a bridge to move forward?

Are we willing to be inconvenienced to help others?

Should the people who are abused fight back with hate or love?

Do we want to, or have to, adjust our lives to oppression?

In our quest for freedom, where does complacency fit? What does the word "perseverance" mean to us?

Isn't fear the greatest fear? Do we fear, or are we free from fear? Isn't it true that only when we are free of fear can we really know freedom?

When we think of injustice or any other type of wrong, is our reaction to assist the person, family, community or nation wronged? Or does the size of the injustice and who it affects, determine our action? Don't the realities of injustice occur not only in third-world countries and other nations, but in our very homes? Isn't it true that wherever injustice occurs, we are affected because we are one?

Does confusion rest just with us, or is it indeed worldwide?

Who will courageously go to battle, in the heart and the mind, for truth? Are we cautious or courageous? Is caution a disguise for weakness?

As we seek truth and justice, are we willing to risk criticism?

Why do we let the conspiracy of silence among some leaders and people continue to damper the hope of those who are feeling the pains of injustice? Isn't the conspiracy alive? Doesn't it continue to grow among the leaders and the people?

In order to tear down our differences with other nations, don't we need to tear down our own discrepancies first? Aren't nations and people the same?

Are we afraid of showing our feelings? Are we afraid of being hurt?

Do we recognize our full potential? Do we push ourselves to our potential? Or are we afraid to risk? Or is risk the very thing that lifts us out of our shell to make a difference? Does responsibility lead to risk, and risk to success?

Isn't it true that each one of us lives risk differently and each one of us can make a difference? Are we willing to dare and do?

What does it take, short of war or a major depression or some other disaster, to awaken the people to step up, speak out and act? Why have we chosen to kill one another? Doesn't the effort to love have to be made in order to create a society inspired by God through love? Can we go back in time and find events where the general public has been aroused and rallied behind an issue and change didn't occur?

Is the name of God held in contempt among the nations?

Isn't now the time for us to be aware, to give input and be active? Can our system of love work with a silent people? Doesn't the opportunity to speak await us now? How many of us know what the leaders in the systems have in store for us? How many of us care?

Haven't we created enough documents with all the right words to fight human rights violations ten times over? Then why are human rights still abused? Does killing trees, to manufacture paper, solve the world's problems?

Are we reluctant to speak and act out of a spiritual base for fear that we might be dubbed religious fanatics?

Are we an aloof people? Do we make half a commitment? Do we live half a life? How can we be content with mediocrity?

If we seek, find and accept truth won't we change our political, social and economical conditions for the better? How can we find and accept truth and not act?

Do the institutions beat us with silence? Don't they ignore protest with silence? Is that reason enough for us to roll over and play dead? Can't we rise again and again and again until we wear them down?

Isn't nuclear destruction our common enemy? Are people content now that we have the capability to destroy our entire civilization? How can we find a solution without the power of God our Father to guide us?

Does the message of Christ disturb today's society?

Do we understand that when we create or destroy, we affect not only others, but ourselves?

In order to change the things with which we are not content, don't we need to go out on a limb?

If we are to be active in change, aren't we better off not depending on results? But only keeping focused on the mission?

Does our silence contribute to injustice? Where has courage gone?

If we are in Christ, isn't it then we can say, "for when I am weak is when I am strong"?

When we tackle the job that's before us, isn't that when we need an unshakable faith? Are we frightened because we have a lack of faith?

How can we exist without a vision? Are our minds and hearts closed?

What good is it to win in all aspects of life but lose in the simple act of love?

If Christ came today, would he find any faith on earth? Are we relentlessly beat up by those who we allow to beat us up?

Do we have the courage to confront and ask meaningful questions when we meet with the hierarchy and leaders?

Once we have done our best, shouldn't we stand firm and God will do the rest?

If we saw the faces of the refugees, especially those of the children, would we cry tears of joy or sadness? If we cry tears of joy, is it because we recognize them as our brothers and sisters? If we cry tears of sadness, is it because they are our brothers and sisters? But in the eyes of the children, don't we see hope?

Isn't it true that in every trial we face, we will not be tested beyond our own strength?

Is there a coordinated conspiracy that objects to good?

Can a civilization without peace be a civilization?

ALL forms of injustice are met with silence at times. The conspiracy of silence needs to be broken anytime it violates any person's right. We cannot sit back and do nothing and wait for something to happen that could be detrimental to our futures. We cannot be timid or inactive. We need to be bold and accept our responsibility to risk and speak out. I believe the time is now to leave our cocoons of comfort and confront the system. In order to be effective, we need to work together and get involved. We need to respond out of love and risk inconvenience in order to break the conspiracy of silence. Let us show our courage.

CHAPTER 6

Man-Made Rules and Regulations

I declare a Revolution to overthrow the following powers of Darkness and to rebuild them with the commandment of love and the living God as cornerstone, through a fusion of the heart and mind. I declare a Revolution to overthrow and rebuild all or any part of any religious and secular institutions, philosophies and organizations *where man-made religious rules and regulations instituted by cowardice create fear and distort and eliminate growth in the spirit of truth in all people.*

I, FOR ONE, ASK:

Why impose rules and regulations and make things difficult for those seeking God? Why do we place heavy burdens on people?

Are we hypnotized by the laws of religion?

Has the institutionalized church grown stubborn, is it acting worse than its ancestors?

Do the higher authorities make their decisions in the cold dark of night, or in the light of day?

Do we obey people rather than God?

Is the true meaning of Christianity and the other great religions obscured by their leaders?

If we say we accept all, why do we discriminate?

How do we react to fear? Do we panic?

Why do organized religions at times seem jealous and ruthless and look like they are only interested in self-preservation? Are they trying to increase their power? Or are they trying to increase their control? Or both?

In some churches, are the doctrines only human regulations?

If the reality is Christ, should we let someone else decide what we should eat or drink, or whether we are to observe annual festivals or the sabbath?

Isn't God life? Isn't he love and truth? Isn't he the light? How can we think of him as an object to worship? Isn't it true that our very movements are his?

Should religions treat those who, in their judgment, are not of their flock as second-class citizens? Shouldn't every church treat non-members the same as members?

If there is eternal life, why do we have a fear of dying?

Do we get all caught up in philosophy? Do we philosophize instead of just accepting? Is it because it's safe?

Isn't life an indivisible whole?

When we serve either our religion or nation, are we careful that we don't inflict harm to others in the process?

Is there really an unknown, or do we have an abundance of hidden knowledge?

What does "In God We Trust" really mean?

Isn't it true that God gives us an incredible power?

Are we afraid to support, acknowledge and encourage the spiritual truths among all people?

What is more important, rules or love?

Why, if religion is not a profession, does the Church use the word "laity"?

Has religion become pathetic?

Isn't Jesus Christ the world's greatest non-conformist?

How can we live without faith? If we have faith, why do we live the way we do?

How can we get the most out of a religious service? Doesn't our attitude affect the result?

If there is evil, who will win the tug-of-war for our hearts? Don't we have a part to play in that tug-of-war?

Man-Made Rules and Regulations

Is it true that we rationalize everything we do?

Do we practice what we preach? Do we place guilt trips and burdens on people without helping them? Do we like to attract attention and take the place of honor at gatherings?

Is a new world in the making? Are we in the midst of a great transformation?

Have we fallen for the white flag of surrender because we have been fed the line of "what can we do, we have no choice, we can't fight the structure, there is no alternative"? If so, isn't that the tragedy of our time?

Before we believe, do we need irrefutable proof?

Doesn't simplicity cut through the "fat" of complexity?

Before we act, do we think we need to do it all, or are we willing to become part, no matter how small?

Do we need to unlearn before we can learn?

Why do we act out the rule, "out of sight, out of mind"?

What can we do on a daily basis to enhance our self-esteem? Wouldn't knowing we are children of God help?

Isn't it true that there is power in internal imagery for healing?

Are we liberated? Liberated in the heart and mind?

If each of us tries to put on Christ, won't the whole world benefit?

When it comes to prejudice, does religion single out women?

Shouldn't we be tolerant of everyone, or are we only tolerant to those who can help us?

Doesn't God promise us inner peace, a peace that we cannot achieve by ourselves?

Do we walk by sight and not by faith? Isn't faith the risk we need to take when we interact with society? If we can see it, how can it be faith?

Isn't all that God our Father asks of us is that we do the best we can?

Man-Made Rules and Regulations

Shouldn't we take what has been given us as a gift, the gift of life, and use it to the maximum?

Are we in self-imposed shackles?

Does the environment shape us, or can we shape it?

Isn't it all right to be angry with cause?

Is there hope for the children, or have we fed them negative thinking that makes survival unlikely?

Why is it difficult for us to believe in peace? Is it because we believe in revenge? Is it because of history?

Does religion contribute to peace or war?

Why, if there are so many denominations that preach the same Jesus Christ, are there so many that claim the only way to Christ?

What is the measuring rod of life—peer approval or God approval?

Aren't we measured by our performance? Does that provide the pressure to turn us away from taking a risk?

Shouldn't we be counting our blessings? Don't they out-weigh the negatives? Shouldn't we thank God our Father with a grateful heart?

Are people on the quest for God? Isn't it true that God is on the quest for all people?

Isn't God's word a living word? Do we find it in a book or in the people, or both?

If we are deceptive, aren't we self-deceptive?

Could it be that the more knowledge we gain, the further away we get from our destiny?

When we analyze the message of Jesus Christ, do we find anything that is impossible to do? Are his messages part and parcel of society, or are they outside in some never-never land? Didn't Jesus Christ suffer? Wasn't he neglected? Didn't he lead the way? Doesn't he live?

Man-Made Rules and Regulations 65

How many of us set admirable goals to change society and to live better, but get derailed because of a lack of commitment, a lack of persistence? Why not say to God, "here I am, send me"?

Is our religious system so organized that it gives us a place to rebel and an excuse to rebel?

Does Christ challenge the conscience of all people or just a select few?

If God forgives us, do we forgive ourselves? Isn't it true that once we forgive ourselves, we can forgive others? When we forgive, do we forget? Can we really forget, or is it just being human to remember?

Isn't it true that guilt or worry can bring sickness?

Is there room for rationalization in faith?

If we reach the heart of our own faith, haven't we reached the heart and faith of others?

Doesn't God our Father deal with us in the "real world"? If so, why not lean on him to make things happen?

Hasn't God our Father reconciled the world to himself? If so, why do we batter each other around?

Isn't it true that through our actions with each other and the experiences we share together, that hearts will open to the truth? Isn't it true that the truth is that God the Father, Jesus Christ and we are one? If so, do we really need law to dictate our actions? Are we ready to accept our responsibility?

If people do not practice the same religion as we do, do we want to convert them out of love or out of fear? Are we so unsure of our own faith that we crave to have everyone think like we do?

Do we enjoy the recognition and respect given by those we meet? Is that what fills our life?

Do we make the "requirements" to enter the kingdom so burdensome and complicated that we "scare" away a large segment of the population? And if they come to listen further, do we lose them forever?

Didn't Christ say, "Anyone who is not against us is for us"?

Do we have to accept dogmatic answers? Isn't it all right to question and challenge?

Man-Made Rules and Regulations

Are we afraid to make a decision in religious communities unless it conforms to man-made law?

Are fundamentalism and fanaticism one in the same? Or only sometimes?

Is there any reason to have a militant religious movement? Isn't that contrary to the message of love?

What can come of infamous laws and tyrannical decrees except hurt?

Can we educate the world to love peace? Isn't peace through reconciliation? From words to actions?

When we hear "our highest self," doesn't that mean the Christ within?

When we hear the word "transformation," do we think personal or global? When transformation takes place, is it then that we are in harmony with ourselves?

What about the power of Christ? Why not test it?

WHEN we recognize the truth, that God the Father, Jesus Christ and we are one, we will also realize that we are free. We can then grow in the Holy Spirit, shedding fear and gaining greater clarity in our life decisions. We will become more sensitive in all our actions, knowing we directly affect each other. I believe that in order for us to be removed from man-made rules and regulations, we need to accept, out of love, our responsibility. Then we will know what we are free not to do, as we fulfill our mission on Earth.

CHAPTER 7
Hypocrisy

I declare a Revolution to overthrow the following powers of darkness and to rebuild them with the commandment of love and the living God as cornerstone, through a fusion of the heart and mind. I declare a Revolution to overthrow and rebuild all or any part of any religious and secular institutions, philosophies and organizations *where hypocrisy permeates, confuses, deforms and smothers the spirit of brotherhood and sisterhood toward one another and clouds the real meaning of life and the destiny of all people.*

I, FOR ONE, ASK:

Where has sincerity gone? Have we replaced it with pretense?

Why has hypocrisy crept into religion?

Why do we find, when we interact with some of the institutionalized churches, that everyone is so preoccupied with worldly matters and politics that it is difficult to keep their attention on spiritual matters?

Does evil disguise itself in pretention?

What is it that intimidates us? Is it the power of the system?

Why do certain religions or Christian institutions think they have the only truth?

Where has the sensitivity of true religion gone?

Isn't it true that money cannot buy what God has given for nothing?

Isn't it true that the kind of worshiper God the Father wants is one who will worship in spirit and truth?

In the quest for freedom, can we leave self-pity, frustration, failure and fear behind us?

Isn't it true that no church or religion should lock people out? Shouldn't they instead open their hearts? What keeps us from opening our arms to others without condition?

Should any church stand in the way of the grace of God, who has made salvation possible for the entire human race?

How can we separate any aspect of life if all things came into being through the living God?

In religion, shouldn't one speak for God and not self?

Doesn't the word "repent" mean change? Hasn't that been the battle cry for years, "repent, repent!"? If we change our thought patterns and love our God and our neighbor as ourselves, with all our heart, soul, mind and strength, won't that in fact change the world?

Why do we keep judging according to appearances? Shouldn't our judgment be according to what is right and what is truth?

If we have really died with Christ to the principles of this world, why do we still let rules dictate to us as though we were still living in this world?

Aren't we blessed with the gift of free will?

Isn't it a good idea always to look inside, just in the event the fault is partly ours?

Can we look beyond the person to the injustice?

Can we really be separate from our neighbor?

Are we tired of all the speeches?

Isn't it true that what we think is what we become?

What do suspicious people think? Or do they think?

Do we look at things differently when they don't concern us? Don't they concern us?

Can we recognize our own weaknesses? Do we see the same weakness in others? Is that what causes us to react? If we are led astray, do we fret and give up on ourselves?

Can we and do we consider others inferior to ourselves?

Hypocrisy

What is the difference between what we could do and what we do?

Where have all the things that man has accomplished gone? Have we advanced toward the light?

Has hate grown up so that it has now become an acceptable part of life?

When we have to interact with someone who is cold and/or arrogant, does it change our normal disposition?

How do we find our way, and help others find their way, through the dark alleys of life?

Why be ambiguous? Is it so we can blend into the shadows? Where does that get us?

Can we really be dissatisfied with life so that we act indifferent, or do we act indifferent because we are satisfied with life?

Does the measure of our intellect help us understand the meaning of life?

In the quiet of a room, with another person, involved with another religious doctrine, do we admit spiritual unity or do we prefer to pray that the other person believe as we do? When people say that we are narrow-minded, they don't mean us, do they?

Do we buy our way out of a situation with a check?

What good is pity for others, without action? Are pain and agony relieved with sympathy?

Can't we envision a world free of injustice? Shouldn't we let our imagination run free, free from the shackles of the status quo?

Have we built a society based on illusion or reality?

If we encounter a setback, do we withdraw inside of ourselves, or do we use the lesson as a stepping stone to future experiences?

What have some of the institutionalized churches done to the name of Jesus Christ?

How exciting can it be to have a fatalistic philosophy?

Can anything separate us from the love of God?

Do we consider optimism unbelievable, or do we accept it as a responsibility?

Do we teach that the human is a total person and that one's ability to fulfill his or her destiny depends on his or her understanding of it?

How can we speak of love outside of the educational institutions and then expect our children to grow up understanding the depth of the challenge?

Are we stuck in a whirlpool of convolutions?

Do we have to wait until a crisis affects our lives or the lives of others before we act?

Why do we argue about words that are meaningless?

Is there a way we can speak of God to people and eliminate the fear of conversion?

Do we wish that things were different now, or have we always wished that things were different?

Even though it's an old thought, do we give thanks daily to God our Father, for the blessings he gives us now and for his promises for the future? Even the things we take for granted?

Don't we, as a people, have the ability to shape our future?

Do we stop long enough to listen? Do we listen with patience and with sincerity?

Do we see ourselves handicapped in viewing the obstacles that we need to overcome? Don't we at times feel inadequate or inferior when we are faced with the responsibility of shaping our society? Are we lured by the illusion created by some people?

Isn't Jesus Christ sending us into the world to make it more human and more divine?

Has Jesus Christ become a sentimental ornament in our lives? Is he a hero of the underdog, but only in the past? Isn't he among us daily, urging us to stay strong with love?

Are we so focused on the outside, looking for the forces of evil, that we don't look within?

Hypocrisy

When we obtain freedom, do we still apply self-control?

Don't we need to cultivate good? Doesn't faith transcend reason?

Do we at times get overwhelmed with life situations? Aren't the trials we face designed by us? Isn't what's important how we act in those trials?

Shouldn't we come to a clear understanding of our strengths as well as our weaknesses?

Can we approach everyone with trust? Does everyone include our adversaries?

Where and why do Holy wars begin and end? Doesn't the thought of it make you sick?

Can we sit back and fire away with words of piety and think we are above reproach?

Hasn't God our Father forgiven our sins and will not call them to mind again, ever again?

Do some in religion use force and fraud as a tool to entrap the people? Is this legalized violence? Does it cause misery? Is this what we call hypocrisy?

Are we a stubborn people always resisting the Holy Spirit?

Should we depend on human wisdom or the power of God?

WE cannot find peace as long as we live a life of hypocrisy. The sad thing is that in the end, it affects not only those directly involved in this deceitful act, but all people. Let us be who we are, children of the living God our Father and not be fitted with the disguise of deception. I believe we need to use love to remove the clouds of hypocrisy and shed light on the real meaning of life and the destiny of all people.

CHAPTER 8

Law of Love

I declare a Revolution to overthrow the following powers of darkness and to rebuild them with the commandment of love and the living God as cornerstone, through a fusion of the heart and mind. I declare a Revolution to overthrow and rebuild all or any part of any religious and secular institutions, philosophies and organizations *which, rather than living the law of love, exploit humankind by butchering fundamental freedoms for their own self-gain, resulting in all forms of tyranny and injustice to all people.*

I, FOR ONE, ASK:

Is it true that our thoughts and emotions which bring forth stress, fear, hate, resentment and jealousy, can cause illness? Shouldn't we will our minds with creative healthy thoughts, rather than negative thoughts?

Why do we act against the dictate of our conscience's? What do we, as a people, gain out of violence in all forms?

Why do we do what we do to one another? Is our own self-preservation the most important thing?

When we attend a prayer breakfast or a religious gathering of any kind, can't we feel the love permeate the room? Can we walk out of that gathering and greet the first person we meet with the same intensity of love, not knowing what his or her religious preference is, if any?

Isn't it true that love is so subtle that it goes unnoticed until it is no longer there? Isn't it true that where love is, God is?

Isn't the way of Christ a way of peace, a way of love so that we may have life and have it to the full? Isn't it far better to give with love without expecting anything in return?

In life's journey, shouldn't we keep the balance of life and not forget the responsibility of the simplest of tasks?

How many times do we need to be told we are free before we believe it?

Does it take steel courage or just a love filled heart to show generosity to our enemies?

Do we depend on a historical God? Do we worship a God of history, or a living God who bears the trials and tribulations of our very own lives every moment of every day?

How can we create an atmosphere of peace around us? Can we do so without the presence of the living God our Father? Isn't it true that nothing will stop the love of God?

Is it true that our outward freedom will come to be only when we achieve inner freedom?

What is the best diplomacy, if not love? Isn't it true that love is the highest expression of the soul?

Isn't our test in the navigation of our lives held in the roughest of seas? Shouldn't we show each other our worth by showing that our ship will hold and not break at the seams in the roughest of waters?

If we don't believe we can create a society inspired by God through love, can it happen? Isn't the choice up to us? Can't each of us make a difference?

What happens to us when we speak from the heart? Do we expose a part of us we would rather keep veiled?

What are we doing that can destroy our relationship with God?

Where do we stand in times of challenge and possible controversy?

If we are one, how can we not risk for the welfare of others?

When we think back on the struggles that have taken place on earth, weren't they struggles between good and evil?

Do we treat shattered dreams with despair? Or do we hope for the next dream? Should we ever give up on hope?

When we march against injustice, shouldn't we be armed only with the weapons of love? Isn't that his way? Isn't love the true conqueror of injustice?

Can we approach our adversary without an agenda of conversion, power or revenge and just love?

Shouldn't our life be without despair? Shouldn't our life be filled with hope, joy, challenge, risk and adventure?

Isn't it true that if all people lived out the reality of love, the true reality of love, that conflict would disappear?

Do we challenge our God-given abilities to the edge?

When we help one another, doesn't that give us a sense of satisfaction and deep-down pleasure?

Do we stop ourselves with our own doubt about our abilities, or is the biggest obstacle fear? Is it fear of failure or fear of success?

Doesn't Christ have a love for us that is beyond comprehension, an unconditional love, that led him to the cross? Doesn't he call us his friends? Didn't he lay down his life for us? If we are friends of Christ, why would we be slaves to anybody or anything?

How can we love others and be happy, optimistic and content if we don't love ourselves first? Can we love ourselves without condition?

When we hear "and this too shall pass," doesn't that say to us that failure and victory are fleeting?

Is it courage that allows us to speak of love in a direct, simple manner that reaches everyone? Is there something wrong with the word love?

Why shouldn't we in all areas of adversity, especially the most difficult ones, approach the solution process with the one enduring solution . . . love? Isn't the method of love to find our way with natural harmony among nations, religions and, in fact, all people?

Why do some in the scientific community react negatively to the words "love," "faith" and "God"? Is it because these words are not complicated enough?

If the message of the gospel is love, why do we treat it with apathy?

Does responsibility mean dependency on one another? Will we accept or evade our responsibility? Does the heart match our actions?

Isn't it true that out of suffering comes compassion? Isn't it true that we cannot escape suffering? Yet isn't suffering a healer?

Why not be in harmony with all people? Unite our energy? Unite our visions? Unite all with love?

What is the greatest test of our faith? Is it when we are beset with trouble and sickness, or prosperity and generosity?

If we say evil, do we think folly? If we think folly, how do we fight individual and institutional evil?

How can our decision to spend money on our war machines and to waste our commodities be justified while one person remains hungry or homeless?

Aren't the dignity and equal rights of all members of the human family the foundation for freedom, justice and peace? Do we believe that together we can accomplish great works, as we all travel life's journey from "cradle to grave"? Isn't the key that we have to believe? If our dream of a just society is to come to be, shouldn't we live, work and dare others to change hearts and live love? Don't we have to believe that by trying, we are going to make things happen?

Is truth something we study and acknowledge, or is truth action?

Isn't it an exciting possibility to join Jesus Christ in his battle for truth? How can we lose? Can we imagine doing the will of God, which is to imitate Christ in his journey, to bear and endure injustices for his honor, glory and praise?

Do we honor God only with lip service? Are our hearts far away? Isn't it true that the greatest gift we can give God our Father is our love for one another? Shouldn't we live the life of love?

In the fight against injustice, isn't non-violence one of the greatest forces at the disposal of humankind? Can't this approach disarm the strongest of enemies?

Isn't it true that what we do, we do with Christ, for Christ and to Christ?

Do we struggle for power to lead the people rather than to free the people?

Isn't it true that truth is more powerful than all the nations combined?

Didn't Christ eat with "tax collectors and sinners"?

Isn't even patriotism subservient to Christ?

Isn't it a fact that from within the heart comes evil intentions: theft, murder, adultery, deceit, indecency, envy, slander and pride? Doesn't the heart also love?

If we are given a great deal, won't a great deal be demanded of us?

Do we contribute to the problems or the solutions?

Don't we shape the values of our children and those around us by our words and actions?

How can individual spirituality turn into global spirituality? Don't we need to persevere in hardship and be joyful in hope?

Isn't it true that we cannot visualize all that God has prepared for those who love him? Can faith prove the existence of realities that at present remain unseen?

Have we abandoned God our Father or has he abandoned us? How can he abandon himself? Can we only relate to survival? Are we always struggling, always looking for happiness? Why?

Isn't the family the foundation of society? What has happened to the family?

Aren't children the reward of life? Aren't they the hope of the future?

How, with so much energy and love centered towards making this earth great, can there be doubt that we will succeed?

WE are all part of the divine plan to change this world of ours, into a world more human and more divine. We need to risk and accept our responsibility so we can live, love and serve all people without distinction. Christ has led the way in a love relationship with the Father and all people. I believe we need to fill every minute, of every hour, of every day, living and serving God the Father and our neighbor out of love. With love, we can destroy all forms of tyranny and injustice and protect and preserve fundamental freedoms. Let us believe and live the law of love.

CHAPTER 9

Spiritual Bondage, Unity and Truth

I declare a Revolution to overthrow the following powers of darkness and to rebuild them with the commandment of love and the living God as cornerstone, through a fusion of the heart and mind. I declare a Revolution to overthrow and rebuild all or any part of any religious and secular institutions, philosophies and organizations *that have enforced by doctrine, arrogance and power, spiritual bondage which affects all people by blinding them to truth and obstructing unity and their personal freedom to continue their return back home to the living God, Father of all people.*

I, FOR ONE, ASK:

Isn't our journey home challenging and in fact, the greatest love-filled adventure known to mankind?

Why do we treat people like babies when it comes to spiritual matters? Don't we insult their intelligence?

In order to complete our trek homeward, don't we first have to remember that we are not apart, nor can we stand apart, from God our Father, or our roadway will break apart before our very eyes?

To whom do we owe our allegiance, God our Father or man? Have we been fed a distorted vision?

Why do some religions seek exclusive privilege by force?

Why do we keep people tied up in religious dogma rather than setting them free in the spirit? Can exploitation be one reason?

Isn't mystical insight in all of us? Isn't it that very insight that causes us to move forward?

If God is spirit, aren't we spirit, all one and the same for eternity?

Why, in order to satisfy our own appetites for power, do we confuse the simple basics with pious arguments?

Spiritual Bondage

Why are we so arrogant as to believe that we have the only way to Christ?

Why are eternal truths distorted?

Why are we afraid to speak about spiritual matters in public? Is it because we feel inadequate? Are we caught in our own trap of self-guilt or pride? Or is it just not in vogue?

Why, when we say "Jesus Christ," does it cause mixed signals in society, even in religious circles?

Isn't it true that we all came from the one God and he is all and in all? Isn't it true that in God we live and move and exist and that our God is God of the living?

Wouldn't it be interesting to see what people do with true freedom? Doesn't freedom carry responsibility? Isn't it true that freedom does not give a license to act without reason and love?

Isn't it true that when we open our hearts to God, we will penetrate the soul and there in the quiet, rests truth? Does truth frighten the establishment? Are we served our death warrant when we proclaim truth? Does spiritual fidelity rattle the cages of the system? Does it threaten pedigrees, history and tradition?

Shouldn't we listen to our inner voice? Doesn't the Holy Spirit teach and guide us, not only this very moment but until the end of time? Isn't that the way to truth?

Didn't God love the world so much that he gave his only son in sacrifice for our sins, so we can enjoy the journey home to the Father and have eternal life?

Isn't it true that God is spirit and those who worship must worship in spirit and truth? Is it too simple?

If we look, will we see the ever present God? Has God been with us all this time, and we still don't know him? Isn't he the source of life? If the spirit gives life, is it true that the body is fleeting?

Do we want to move with the spirit, or do we want to go another way? If we hear the spirit, will we not leave the hollowness of death, both spiritually and physically and live for eternity?

What is the test of our civilization? Isn't it true that every challenge we face will bring us closer to our destiny?

Where is home? Shouldn't it be in the heart? Shouldn't the heart be in God our Father?

Spiritual Bondage

Is there any reason to undermine what others believe in their spiritual pursuits? Is it because we are unsure of ours?

How can we know another individual's relationship with God? If we are unique and special persons, "one of a kind," doesn't it seem logical, that we will react to our God differently? Even though God is always the same?

Isn't a treasured gift from God our Father, his continued wisdom for us to live out truth? Isn't it true, that in the midst of untruth, truth persists? Aren't we consecrated in truth?

Does life end or begin with death? Is that the question we will ask on our deathbed?

When we hear the word "eternity," what does that mean to us?

When we are overwhelmed by gloom and despair do we sit and rot away, or do we dig down deep to find the warmth of God who comforts and leads us to the light?

Is God a figment of the imagination, or is that what others would like us to believe?

If we are heading towards our destiny, aren't we heading towards the divine?

When we speak of the power within, aren't we really talking about the God within? Are we all not aware of the hidden power that lies within?

Weren't people once made slaves by law or physical means? Are they now enslaved by the power of their positions and the means they use to perpetuate them?

What is the ultimate mystery, the unknown? Do we recognize it deep within our souls? Have we not looked?

If we believe we are one, aren't we responsible to ourselves and to others, and shouldn't that be the same for all people? When we strike out at someone else, don't we realize we are striking out at ourselves? Isn't it true that if we harm just one person in any form, we are in fact harming the entire world?

Shouldn't we live each day of our lives to the fullest? Doesn't the Spirit bring an over abundance of love for us to use freely in the market place of life? Doesn't God give us the energy of life, his energy, to fulfill our mission here on earth?

Aren't we in a long distance run to fulfill our destiny?

How can we not love the truth and Christ, knowing they are from the Father? Aren't Christ and the Father timeless and one? Doesn't truth bring life? Isn't the opposite of truth death by evil, the dark side? When we have light, how can we be drawn into the dark? Isn't it true that the dark side, using the lie as its weapon, destroys by murdering peace of mind and magnifying fears and anxieties? Doesn't it create a domino effect by undermining love, happiness, hope, beauty, kindness, goodness, patience and ultimately truth?

Is it "in" to move with the trend, even if it's against our conscience?

When things are at their darkest, no hope is in sight, and frustration is at a high, isn't it then that the trust we have in God determines our actions?

Is there any way to face impossible odds without knowing that God is in complete control? Can we develop our full potential without faith?

Isn't it true that the real source of power is the Holy Spirit that lives within? Isn't it from the Spirit of Christ imbedded deep in our souls, that we gain our purpose in life? Isn't it then that we become renewed with a vision of hope for all mankind?

Is it possible to unveil the cloak of grey that prohibits us from seeing God the Father within all people?

Is human intelligence suspect? Have we been led to think we're dumb when it comes to spiritual matters?

Can we be insensitive to the cry of another?

How can we deal with the complexity of today's life without compromising our values and dreams?

Don't we need to reach for the cross and embrace it with love, for isn't it the crossover in life that leads to the light? Why not take Christ up on his offer and follow him? Don't we all share in the same struggle of human nature which drags and pulls us away from the light?

Is there any such thing as me and God, or you and God, or me, you and God? Isn't it true that there is no separation, only unity?

Are we molded by the Spirit of Christ or by the spirit of earth?

Can we simply surrender to God and then get on with life? Is it then when we call that he will say, "Here I am"?

Do we ever trust the moment we live in, or are we too busy looking to the future?

Are we fed a continuing plate of impending doom?

Is it true that when we tear the veil from our eyes and the wax from our ears and the muck from our heart, we will know we are one, the truth?

When we speak of the divine within, don't we speak of sharing with God, with Jesus Christ? Isn't that the truth?

Doesn't the miracle of faith elevate us beyond sickness, beyond death?

Who is the alpha and the omega? Isn't it true that it is God our Father? Isn't it true that if it is God, then it is Christ? Isn't it true that if it is Christ, then it is us?

If we had to choose one objective in life, wouldn't it be to seek the truth? Doesn't the truth set us free? And isn't it in that freedom that we find unity?

Who can separate us from the love of Christ? Isn't he always seeking us, even when we are not seeking him?

Can failure out-take and out-capture our confidence if we are rooted in God?

Isn't our soul in constant battle between darkness and light, evil and good? How can we fight the battle if we don't acknowledge it exists?

Are we waiting too long to do? To be? Or are we just waiting to die? When we remember what our purpose is, isn't that when we are ready to do?

Have we forgotten who we are? Are we still looking for ourselves? Are we on a journey to nowhere?

Doesn't the letter of the law kill, and the spirit give life?

Does the type of person we were yesterday, have anything to do with the type we are today? Isn't it true that we have the opportunity to begin a new life not everyday, but every moment?

Doesn't our birthright include inner peace?

Aren't we in a constant state of becoming? Isn't it true that God our Father has not finished us yet?

How can unity in diversity be a goal when it already exits? Is the trouble that we can't recognize it? Aren't we now and forever more a community of one? Aren't we the invisible order of people who are already in place?

What good are satanic cults other than for a one-way ticket to hell?

Have we come to realize that we are a temple, a temple of God with the Spirit of God living in us?

Are we seduced by the pleasure of earth to the point of losing sight of our final destiny?

Isn't the way to the cross the way to the divine within? Wasn't the cross to be the beginning of the journey for all people to return home. Doesn't the cross give eternal life to all people? Isn't it a gift from the son? Wasn't his commitment to the cross a united will between he and the Father? Didn't he know he had come from God and was returning to God?

Isn't the kingdom within? Isn't it in us and among us?

CHRIST has given us a light which eliminates fear, chaos and darkness, and reveals our innermost self, while always illuminating the roadway back home. However, evil gives birth to the lie which produces false doctrine, distorting truth and feeding arrogance, which separates unity through the abuse of worldly power. I believe the fulfillment of our life is to know that we are the light and indeed all children of God. Christ is in us, God the Father is in Christ, and together we are one, the truth. With that knowledge imbedded deep in our souls, nothing will be able to detour us from our journey back home to the living God our Father.

CHAPTER 10
Brick and Mortar

I declare a Revolution to overthrow the following powers of darkness and to rebuild them with the commandment of love and the living God as cornerstone, through a fusion of the heart and mind. I declare a Revolution to overthrow and rebuild all or any part of any religious and secular institutions, philosophies and organizations *where the brick and mortar and other building materials of churches, mosques, temples and other places of worship are for the sake of structure only, using a cornerstone of materialism and/or bankrupt religious spirit which is fruitless and worthless and produces nothing for all people.*

I, FOR ONE, ASK:

Aren't we satisfied with trying the patience of people without trying the patience of God?

Why do we acquire and build buildings or institutions when God wants only compassion? Do the buildings and institutions have love as their cornerstone?

Why do we keep exploiting our own people in many situations?

Shouldn't the institutionalized church and other organizations be likened to a grain of wheat?

If the Holy Spirit took a day off, would the institutionalized church know it?

Why does the institutionalized church at times seem oppressive? Does it take an unchanging rigid stance that is caught in a web of legalism?

Isn't it true that if we change the churches, we can change the world?

Shouldn't some institutionalized churches look inside before their walls crumble like sifted sand?

Do we crave the latest novelty in religion?

Are the vendors fleecing the people?

Do some of the churches carry with them excessive pride built on conceit and arrogance?

Is it true that some institutions and organizations should be ashamed of their conduct but have forgotten how to blush?

Have we rejected the sermon on the mount and grasped the mysteriousness of whatever? Can we hide in the "whatever's"?

Doesn't Jesus Christ challenge the spirit of the world? Doesn't he invite us to come and partake in the challenge?

Do we constantly try to remake ourselves in the image of God? Are we strong enough to probe the unknown?

What measuring rod do we use for success?

Why do some of the religious leaders quarrel with each other, instead of being united?

Shouldn't we have enough humility to confess our errors?

How do we think people who are starving, oppressed and besieged with injustice react to the words, "God and freedom"?

What do competition and religion have in common? Why do we thrive on competition?

Why is it so hard to accept change?

Does the power lie with the human, or with God?

Why do some religious institutions tell people they are free, when by their very nature the institution binds them?

Are we loving or performing in church rituals?

Isn't it true that the most illiterate person can have a deep heartfelt knowledge of faith and truth? Do we try to confuse that person with a list of do's and don't's?

Isn't it true that salvation can be found without the teachings of the institutionalized church?

Why, when we impose our position on a religious matter with others, does it inevitably end in a bitter argument?

Is freedom a word that is all washed up, or can we ignite it with the firepower of God through love?

Isn't it true that in Christ there is no denial of unity?

How can the religions not be concerned with the social and economic conditions of all people?

Are the religions really involved in social justice, or are they paying lip service to placate the people?

How can we follow the way of love in a world possessed with power without the inner strength of the living God our Father?

Doesn't the world consist of little communities that in essence are a total community, a family?

Why are there hostilities among the religions of the world? Is it possible that religions can argue over truth, to the point of war?

When we face the problems of health, housing and food is love part of the solution, or do we assume it's a given?

Is there a difference between religion and spirituality? Doesn't spirituality transcend religions?

Isn't it true that wherever we go, we take ourselves along? Why look to external changes for happiness? Isn't it within that we find the joy of life?

Why do we frustrate ourselves looking for perfection? Do we feel guilty if we relax?

When we live with a cornerstone of self-interest, who really benefits?

Isn't our vivid imagination a good thing, especially when we imagine peace?

What external accomplishments have we had that have led us to a lifetime of joy?

With a lack of vocations in the institutionalized church, is the Holy Spirit trying to tell us something?

Do walls make a church?

Do the institutions grow and grow because big is better? Are we looking for quality or quantity?

Isn't the small act of reaching out one of the most powerful acts we can perform?

Don't people have the ability to turn themselves from the ordinary to the extraordinary?

Is the great social disease the segregation of spirituality from our institutionalized world?

To have peace, don't we need to teach peace and act peace?

Do we have to be superior in our lives, jobs, country and religion? Is that superiority killing us?

Do we want another meeting or study to discuss the last meeting or study and prepare for a new meeting or study? Haven't we completed enough studies without an acknowledgment to the living God?

Is religion a cohesive or divisive force? Does religion promote intolerance?

If we are too imbedded in our religion, do we fear and hate those who differ?

Have we forfeited life so that we live in a shell of nothing?

Is it incompetence, excessive ambition, or just plain tyranny that runs some of our structured entities?

Shouldn't the institutionalized church be a living organism seeking to serve God and people? Has it become secular in its pursuit to perpetuate?

Do we take religion seriously, spiritually seriously?

Do we judge spirituality by the conduct of our churches?

In seeking truth, are we slow-witted? Do we cling to illusion? Isn't it about time that illusion was shattered with the reality of the living God?

Is it possible that we can separate days of worship from days of living? How in the world can we do that, if we are whole? Should worshipping be a chore?

Can the institutions be so blind not to notice that the people are hurting?

Don't we need to resist unjust structures, and seek a way to change them through the power of love?

Doesn't it take both the oppressed and the privileged to change structure?

Isn't it a tragedy that some religions run on ego? Do we make our mark based on the size of our steeples?

Have we reduced religion to a social function?

Are we a stubborn people with our institutionalized hearts, always resisting the Holy Spirit like our ancestors did?

Does the organized church serve only those who have a problem or are a problem?

Do we flaunt our piety? Is it important to others or to ourselves to be very religious?

Are we so preoccupied with appearances that we forget the inner meaning of truth? Are we demented by pride? By self-indulgence?

In order to follow Christ, don't we have to renounce ourselves, take up our cross and follow him?

Isn't forgiveness wonderful?

Do we approach life like a flag flapping in the wind with no direction? Do we follow the crowd?

Has religion become nothing more than a superstition? Are we still selling idols?

Are some in religion more interested in the power of money than in salvation? Do we say "not me"?

Isn't it true that visible things last only for a time, and invisible things are for eternity?

Isn't it true that the Law of God is written in our hearts? If we look deep, won't we see him and understand his teachings? Doesn't the Law of God apply to the weak and uneducated, as well as the strong and educated?

THE living God our Father made the world and everything in it. He doesn't make his home in shrines made by human hands and isn't locked into places and things. We should worship the Father in spirit and truth, for he and we are spirit. The Holy Spirit, who is the life-giver, will teach us everything and remind us all of what has been said, to lead us home. Our places of worship should be living that light, if the Holy Spirit is to interact with us as a community, a community of one.

CHAPTER 11
Power of Guilt

I declare a Revolution to overthrow the following powers of darkness and to rebuild them with the commandment of love and the living God as cornerstone, through a fusion of the heart and mind. I declare a Revolution to overthrow and rebuild all or any part of any religious and secular institutions, philosophies and organizations *which perpetuate themselves through the power of guilt, greed, false teaching and secrecy, causing resentment, anger, and paranoia, which corrode like gangrene in all people.*

I, FOR ONE, ASK:

Do some in organized religion measure everything they do with a bottom line of profit, whether it be money or other things that can be identified with numbers? Why has money, rather than human resources, become the driving force in our institutions? Is it for power?

Why is it necessary to hold closed-door meetings when it comes to religion? What can be so secretive about religion that we have to keep it from the people? Isn't secrecy the enemy of freedom?

Why do we worry about how to self-perpetuate rather than strive to work ourselves out of a job?

What is it that keeps us from opening our arms to those that are outside of what we think?

Why are we so possessive of our faith?

Why do we go around offering the word of God for sale? Do we think that religion is a way of making a profit? Why do we let profit dictate our conscience?

Why at times do we teach a doctrine that complicates? Is it because we are full of self-conceit?

Doesn't the institutionalized church need to affirm its people? Doesn't it need to assure them of their love and support? Doesn't it need to thank the people for their assistance?

Why does the church place guilt trips on people and barter with them through intimidation?

Why do some institutionalized churches insult and intimidate people by their methods to collect funds?

Has institutionalized religion grown rich and powerful, fat and slick, and is it now looking to exploit?

Doesn't false teaching of any kind corrode like gangrene?

Have we, one more time, used the house of the Lord as a market to sell our products?

Isn't there a great truth in the statement, "Let the one among you who is sinless be the first to throw a stone"?

Does keeping things secret give us a comfort zone?

What about our divine powers?

Where do selfishness and materialism lead?

In dealing with people, is our method coercion?

Is life a roller-coaster ride? Does it cause anxiety and fear or joy?

Shouldn't we have a personal relationship with God our Father? When we are in-tune with God, do we find greater energy and happiness?

Who are the criminals? Who are the leaders? Who are the servants? Who are the hypocrites?

Are we so proud of tradition that it paralyzes us in looking toward the future?

Why are we not content with the knowledge that leads us to truth? Can wisdom that is founded in truth be challenged by reason? Doesn't truth triumph over untruth?

Isn't it true that if someone is hurting, we hurt too, and if someone is joyous, we too are joyous?

Who doesn't want, and who shouldn't be working towards, peace?

Isn't it true that when we acknowledge and recognize that we have a little good and a little bad in each of us, we will come to recognize the good in all?

Is it difficult to be content in whatever state of mind we are in? Where can we gain the strength to be content? What does contentment have to do with logic?

Are we so caught up and frustrated in looking ahead and so unsatisfied with the present that we have ignored our accomplishments of the past?

Do the institutions know how to relate to the common person?

Aren't we truly blessed to have so many people in society concerned with all the components that make up life?

Do we look for bargaining positions before we act?

Isn't it true that we all form one community, headed for one common destiny?

Have we lost sight of who we are? Don't we all look to a religion to solve the riddle of life?

Isn't it true that low self-esteem drains us of our talents and builds on insecurity? How can we find joy if we don't like ourselves?

Does stress eventually lead to violence?

Have we really reflected on all of our assets to see how they apply to every aspect of our lives?

When we are faced with a negative situation, do we see it as an opportunity?

Do we do things for money, or do we do them because we enjoy them?

Do we dehumanize ourselves?

Are we at the end of the road or the end of our intellectual detour?

Can we look to the institutions to provide us peace, or is that really the impossible dream?

Aren't the most treasured gifts without a price?

Are we frank to the point of being cruel? Do we need to have the upper hand?

Are we confident to the point of being arrogant?

If we are preoccupied with the material things that life brings, do we sacrifice our relationship with God our Father?

Why do some, in religion, build a kingdom within a kingdom making a mockery out of their religion?

Are the lonely and elderly, who hope and pray, hunted by some in religion?

How can we "find" ourselves without God our Father? How can we seek the divine, without knowing that we, as a people, are united?

Do we hold, or are we fed, a gloomy and pessimistic view of the future?

Shouldn't we live as though each day is our last? If we lived like this, then wouldn't we approach everything differently? What makes us think that this is not our last day?

Do we spend hours upon hours seeking religious formulas to solve society's ills? Haven't we theorized peace to a pulp? Don't we need action . . . action rooted in love?

If we prepare for war, will we get war or peace? If we prepare for peace, will we get peace or war? Isn't the choice to love or hate, to wage war or to make peace?

Are we so self-righteous that we fail to look within?

Is it easier to deny the truth, than to partake? Isn't it easy to get so caught up in ideas and slogans that we forget why we were doing what we were doing?

Isn't it true that the spirit of Christ is undefeatable in any action?

Do we teach how to preach, recruit and raise money or to love and serve?

By our actions, do we undermine the faith of others? Do we win if our gain causes the ruin of another?

When we self-surrender to God, don't we have to strip ourselves of self, so we can be fully open to him?

Have the institutions complicated the message of Christ? Why would they do such a thing? Isn't Christ's message easy to understand and act out?

When we are in tune with God, isn't the direction we're heading in life firmly established? Shouldn't we be living our lives for the one who sacrificed himself for us?

Who is able to harass us with worry and despair, blow things out of proportion and disturb all the fibers of our souls? Who is able to give us hope and light, courage and strength, keep things in focus and give us peace?

Isn't the bottom line love and unity?

Before we believe, do we demand a sign?

Can we buy God off with the accepted tithing of 10%?

Why use desperation as inducement? Do some in institutionalized religion appeal to those who have soft hearts? Is begging or whining in vogue?

What would Jesus Christ think, say and do if he attended all the religious conventions?

Do smugness, greed, pomp, hypocrisy and exploitation have anything to do with some in religion? Have some confused and violated the public trust? Have we turned the house of God into a bandit's den?

Why not try selling snake-oil? Will it generate enough income to build the next church or theme park?

Is our faith like a leaky sink that holds no water?

Do we frivolously look to change religion for what's "in" today? Isn't it a fact that anybody who is convinced that he or she belongs to Christ must reflect that we all belong to Christ, no more than the other?

Do we let guilt paralyze us? If we are forgiven by the all-forgiving God, why fall prey to the trap?

Do we seek the latest craze and novelty one after the other, always curious, learning and exploring, but somehow not coming to the knowledge of the truth? Will we turn to myths rather than truth?

THE time has come for us to reject anyone or anything that places a guilt trip on us. Further, we need to combat greed with generosity and replace paranoia with trust, secrecy with openness, anger with love and false teachings with truth. I believe only we can allow things like resentment, anger and paranoia into our lives, and only we can allow love in to cleanse our hearts, minds and souls so we can spread our light throughout the world.

CHAPTER 12

Word and Deed

I declare a Revolution to overthrow the following powers of darkness and to rebuild them with the commandment of love and the living God as cornerstone, through a fusion of the heart and mind. I declare a Revolution to overthrow and rebuild all or any part of any religious and secular institutions, philosophies and organizations *which employ and accept the discrepancy between word and deed and the crippling of the spirit of life for self-preservation, causing frustration, mistrust, and hate in all people.*

I, FOR ONE, ASK:

Why do we persist in changing words and deeds so they never mesh?

Why are we so caught up in being number one? Where has love gone?

Isn't the weakness of churches, nations and people the discrepancy among word, creed and deed?

Can life go on with the civilized conditions to which we have been accustomed?

Is deception one of our better resources?

Why, at times, do we hear empty lectures rather than love and compassion from the pulpit?

Does the word "inconsistent" mean anything to you?

Do we foolishly undertake a change of course?

Why can't we begin with trust instead of looking immediately for the hidden agenda?

If there is a God, then shouldn't we, when times are rough, put our trust in him, and not be afraid?

Why is it difficult to speak out about Jesus Christ in conversation and not with preachy attitudes?

Why when we hear the word "sin," do we recoil?

Is it difficult to try to do what always pleases God?

Have we ever thought what it would be like to give of our lives to others, even to the point of death?

Have we loved or judged our neighbor?

In our search for truth, what do we do with anger, hatred and prejudice?

Can we, as a nation, really interact with the rest of the people of this planet? Why is there an ongoing power struggle?

Do we do the things we want to do, or do we have to do the things we don't want to do? Do we understand our own human weaknesses?

Where is there a conflict of interest? Do we think before we act?

How can we sit still and not put our ideas into action?

Is it hard for us to ask forgiveness of God and our neighbor?

Where do unkind words and unkind deeds get us? Are we in a "gotcha" mentality?

Have we focused on the world, so it will seduce us with the illusions of materialism and what is "accepted" in our homes, jobs and everyday encounters?

Are religions suspicious of each other's motives?

When we compare east and west, is human nature any different?

Do we handle life with indifference?

Isn't the aftermath of violence lost hope and tragic bitterness?

Do the teachings of doctrine by the religious community help, hinder or eliminate the spirituality they are trying to teach?

Can we say, "Father, forgive them for they do not know what they do"?

Is it true that in order for change to occur we first need to believe that we, the people, together, really can change society?

Are we confused? Do we believe that peace can only come through violence and conquest?

How can we change anything without the power of God our Father?

Can we separate the moral and ethical obligations that we instill in each other as individuals, from institutions and organizations?

Why, when we are so caught up in power and tradition, do we think peace is a fantasy?

If we think positive, can we be cancelled out by those who think negative?

Can we at least agree not to kill each other?

If we don't care about ourselves, shouldn't we care about the children?

Is the true test of human beings their words or their actions or both?

Do we need to be concerned with what other people think about us? Why not just say, "so what"?

Is it possible to wait until everything is right before we seek change? Isn't this the time to change?

Do we have memories of convenience?

When we compromise, do we compromise our character? Do we compromise the will of God in our service to the institutions and nations? Are we living a contradiction?

If we have stumbled along the way, why not recognize it rather than disguise it? If we recognize it, doesn't it make sense that we can correct it? Isn't each trial an opportunity to grow in God and self?

Isn't self-interest, in any form, counterproductive? Does the word, "interdependency" mean anything to you?

Isn't the knowledge we seek for a better world, already within, through the Holy Spirit? Why not reflect and commit?

Is it pure foolishness to love our enemies?

Who is the common person? Is he the one who hears, sees and understands with his heart? Wasn't Jesus with the common person?

Is it true that some of the trivial things we face are the solutions to the big issues?

Doesn't the same God who gives us life, give us liberty?

Isn't it true that when we seek change, we need to wrap ourselves with courage and confidence?

We say peace, but do we want peace? Who survives a conflict? Who benefits from a conflict? Aren't we tired of conflict? Why don't we bury it with peace? What is our choice, survival or extinction?

Have we confused activity with results? How can we improve without the living God working in our lives?

Isn't it true that Jesus Christ was a man for others?

Isn't it true the only way to really love God is by our love for one another? Doesn't that say something to us? Don't we need to trust and surrender to God our Father?

Isn't it true that if we claim to love God and hate our neighbor, we are a liar? Isn't our neighbor everyone?

Don't we brutalize one another in the name of unity?

Do we act against social injustice only if it affects us? Do we realize that at times we react only when we're individually threatened? But aren't we always affected?

Who is our family? Isn't it the people of the world?

Do we make speeches, hold seminars and shuffle papers from one end of the conference table to the other, thinking we have moved a light year? Is that an illusion or reality?

Are our minds twisted with rhetoric? Are doubts stirring in our hearts?

Have we, as yet, learned the art of communication? Is the door open for dialogue?

Who is responsible for controversy and divisiveness, the people or the leadership? Aren't they the same?

Do we have meetings to determine answers to our problems or only to establish the time for the next meeting?

Does the Bible unite us or divide us?

Doesn't our God the Father hear us if we groan?

Can the God we know create an earth that is full of chaos?

Do we prostitute ourselves for gain?

Isn't Christ everything and in everything?

Are some of the speeches we hear a cover for trying to get money?

Do we commit crimes against the sacredness of life?

THERE was no discrepancy by Christ between his word and deed. He proved his words by his deeds. We have the same opportunity to create a vision of love and never let go. We, as a people, at some point, come to the realization that human life is truly an ongoing process. Every day of our lives brings different challenges filled with opportunities and problems as we interact with one another. We have the responsibility to take advantage of our opportunities and face our problems, not to condemn them, but to solve them. I believe that through love, we can remove frustration, mistrust and hate by matching our words with our deeds as we live out our lives to the fullest.

CHAPTER 13

Disunity

I declare a Revolution to overthrow the following powers of darkness and to rebuild them with the commandment of love and the living God as cornerstone, through a fusion of the heart and mind. I declare a Revolution to overthrow and rebuild all or any part of any religious and secular institutions, philosophies and organizations *that cause disunity among people and discriminate either in race, color, sex, religion, or national origin, generating turmoil and barbarous acts at the expense of all people.*

I, FOR ONE, ASK:

If we don't believe that all people are created equal, why not rip out the pages that say so from the Declaration of Independence, The Universal Declaration of Human Rights, The Bible and other legal and sacred documents?

How can torture be justified for any means?

Do we take advantage of those who have less than we have?

How can governments commit murder to obtain their self-taught principles?

Isn't unity only possible when we seek truth? If we find truth, does it do us any good if we don't recognize it and accept it as a gift? In our gifts from God, do we show ingratitude?

Do we look to others for our moral responsibility? Does that take the burden off of us?

How do we think the blood of the people affects the living God?

Does God really reveal himself daily to every human being? Do we have to set up an appointment?

If we are a minority, do we lose heart? Or do we gain courage? What is a minority anyway? Are we reluctant to be identified with a minority idea?

Is non-conformity costly?

What harm can come to us individually, if we slight a single human being? If we are one, don't the successes and failures of everyone affect us?

Shouldn't we be concerned with the culture of others? Don't we really need to keep an open mind?

Do we think that we have an exclusive market on God?

Are we led in the direction of the sound of many voices and forces? Don't our acts determine the nature of the voice we hear?

Is it social respectability, royalty, snobbery or simplicity that sparks life?

Do we ask, "who is my neighbor?" Or do we recognize him or her in all people?

Are we concerned only with our nation, our religious preference and our social status?

Do we see people as a reflection of ourselves or of specific elements, such as nationality, color, sex or religious preference?

Why not the healing power of love?

Isn't it true that if we serve Christ, we will not be wounded by disappointment?

Does it matter how many times we are knocked down in the pursuit for justice? Or truth?

Do we want to go to our graves with the words "if only" on our lips?

What is the common bond that unites all human beings? Isn't it the living God our Father? Then doesn't it stand to reason that if we rupture that bond, we rupture not only us, but God himself?

Shouldn't we educate our children to grow in strength and knowledge of service to others? Is it possible to live not for ourselves, but for others? Do we realize that if we live for others, we also live for ourselves?

Isn't there already in place an invisible army of people armed with the truth of love?

Aren't the faults we see in others just a reflection of our faults?

Do conflict, struggle and sacrifice lead us to our destiny? Isn't suffering, in one form or another, part of life? Doesn't it become our mask of courage?

Isn't it true that the love of the living God our Father excludes no one? Doesn't that include all people, all nations and all religions, even those who do not believe or are adversaries?

Don't we need to love and integrate ourselves with all humankind? Didn't Christ reach for the cross in order to show his love for all humankind? Aren't we responsible for the universe? Is anyone exempt?

Shouldn't we weigh our actions before we consider a choice right or wrong? Do our choices concern only us, or everyone on this earth? Doesn't that mean that every act, good or bad, not only affects the individuals involved, but all people throughout the world? Isn't there a mutual advantage in assisting one another?

Aren't we all scared a little? Why pick at each other? Wouldn't we think at least a little before moving into a glass house? What makes us think we are smug and spotless?

When we are faced with a crisis, do we think that it's the end, a trip to nowhere? Or is a crisis really an opportunity to grow?

Do we use a band-aid mentality when it comes to some global problems? Isn't it true that a band-aid cannot stop a cancer?

Shouldn't we look to the inner person rather than the outer shell?

Isn't the movement towards unity the roadway to peace? Aren't all the pieces in place for creating peace?

Do we live in the grey twilight of complacency? Are we frozen in the muck?

When we hear the word "refugee," does it say to us, a prisoner of sorts, a victim of circumstance?

Shouldn't "prisoners of conscience" be freed? Are we aware of people's disappearances? The missing?

How can we refuse justice to the unfortunate and cheat the poor of their rights?

Isn't it true that Jesus prayed "May they all be one. Father may they be one of us, as you are in me and I am in you"? Wasn't that a prayer of unity in diversity? Isn't it inconceivable that a prayer of hope and not despair by Jesus Christ, to the Father just before the cross of love, was not answered by the Father?

Do we have an unknown God? Isn't the unknown God, the God of all the living, God our Father?

Disunity

By persuading others that we have a right to exist, do we take an overly aggressive attitude of justified abuse toward them? How many people have we battered for justice? Does justice justify violence?

Do we plan for peace or plan to fail, because we have reconciled ourselves to the threat of war?

Isn't it true that there is more international cooperation today than ever before? If so, why do our problems keep intensifying?

Isn't it true that once we accept ourselves, we lose the drive to impress others?

Isn't the gift of freedom that God gives, the gift to be ourselves?

If we speak of reform, is it really reform, or one power group replacing another?

Is it true we know more about killing than living? Don't we have the right not to kill and not to be killed?

Isn't it true that no matter what institution we talk about, all institutions are made up of people? Aren't institutions created for the good of all people? Why else would they be created?

When one says, "the brotherhood and sisterhood of man" what does that mean? Is that the beginning of unity and diversity? Don't we need to be strong in our own faith first and then reach out? Isn't that what unity in diversity is all about?

Isn't God the Father, always present in times of difficulties? When we face trials and persecutions, isn't faith the only thing that can bring us through?

When we talk of bondage, is it self-inflicted by greed, prejudice, fear and anxiety, or do we chose to blame others? Can we really look at situations objectively?

Why can't peace, justice and freedom thrive throughout all the lands? Is it because we really haven't come to grips with the power and believability in the living God our Father who offers us his peace?

Can we escape from reality? Can we live apart from society? Are we starving for food? Are we starving for affection?

If we are free, should we sit back and watch others suffer in chains of different colors, or should we help those in their own plight to be free?

Has our faith been dulled by accepting the "norm"?

If we can give to the best of our abilities, without looking for results but trusting that we have in fact made impact, isn't that faith?

Who are the hungry, thirsty and poor? If there is one person hungry, thirsty or poor, aren't we all?

Do we look beyond the eyes of each other to search the unknown? Do we look outside of our person rather than dig within?

Are we so preoccupied with everything that we concentrate on nothing?

Isn't it true that when we think of the other person first, cooperation for the benefit of everyone takes place?

If we are interdependent with one another, then isn't it time to accept our responsibility to help one another?

Don't our actions create the consequences that can lead to our survival?

Do some of the institutions commit crimes of the heart under the guise of religion or other humanitarian justifications?

Do we have to compare ourselves with others in order to feel superior?

When we are faced with problems, do we see them as our downfall or rise, failure or success? Don't we have, within ourselves, all the resources through the living God to rise and conquer the negative? But don't we first have to accept the responsibility that the problem is ours to solve?

If we avoid our responsibility, do we contribute to havoc?

Shouldn't we surrender our will to Christ, rather than society?

When we speak of harmony, are we afraid to rock the boat? Is harmony with society more important than our destiny?

What do we really have to fear from humankind? Is it color, sex, nationality or race? Or is it power we have to fear?

Don't we need to be a model for one another? If we look deep, don't we all look alike?

If our God is a forgiving God, does that mean our forgiveness of one another will eliminate hate, anger, frustration and anxiety? Doesn't forgiveness, in effect, cause healing, healing of ourselves and others?

THIS earth and its systems have been shaped by people like you and me from all walks of life. Therefore, the power to change society lies with all people. If my country and your country are to become great and grow in love, we cannot be afraid to fight the system if it is wrong. We cannot be afraid to stand up and be counted. As a united people, with love as our weapon, we will be able to stop turmoil and barbarous acts at the expense of all people and eliminate disunity. I believe that with love, we can fire up a unity that is already in place, that transcends all people of all nations, a unity that needs not rituals, dogma or rules and regulations of institutions to be recognized.

CHAPTER 14

The Mountain of Injustice

I declare a Revolution to overthrow the following powers of darkness and to rebuild them with the commandment of love and the living God as cornerstone, through a fusion of the heart and mind. I declare a Revolution to overthrow and rebuild all or any part of any religious and secular institutions, philosophies and organizations *which harbor aggression, injustice, conceit, fanaticism, discrimination, ignorance, manipulation, ruthlessness, repression, contempt, imprudence, apathy, paranoia, rejection, hostility, cynicism, revenge, pride, savagery, lying, arrogance, misrepresentation, lethargy, blasphemy, affliction, hate, slaughter, cheating, endless disputes, anxiety, anger, deceit, resentment, condemnation, prejudice, self-pity, exploitation, hypocrisy, rivalry, distortion, bigotry, violence, slander, spiritual pride, oppression, sorcery, perjury, disharmony, corruption, suspicion, vengefulness, wrangling, torture, callousness, idolatry, jealousy, radicalism, irrespon-*

sibility, pig-headedness, intimidation, hardness of heart, slavery, obstinateness, narrowness, self-centeredness, recklessness, greed, fear, tyranny, rudeness, bribery, indecency, ungratefulness, wickedness, irritation, stubbornness, intolerance, trickery, falsehood, malice, envy, madness, secrecy, militantness, cruelness, feuds, treachery, bitterness, mercilessness, irrationality, spite, mistrust, threats, dishonesty, antagonism, cowardice, defeat, neglect, disillusionment, underhandedness, libel, mindless zealotry, spiritual bondage and any other evil outrage against all people.

I, FOR ONE, ASK:

Do we learn from history, or do we keep repeating the same mistakes over and over again? What has happened to us over the last 2000 years?

Are we doing what God wills each of us to do? Isn't our vocation part of that will? How can we believe in his light and not act? Are we complacent and resigned to our state of affairs? Do we have faith and confidence in our own abilities to succeed in life? What would you do with your life if you knew you couldn't fail?

Why are we so afraid when we hear "New Age"? Are we afraid of primitive religions? What about metaphysical philosophies? Isn't the truth the truth period?

The Mountain of Injustice 145

What about the handicapped, disabled and mentally retarded? Shouldn't we thank God for those who love?

Why do some who have chosen a religious vocation like to get lost in deep questions of dogma?

Are we content with a family, job, home, and all the creative components? Is that all there is?

When we hear "extended family," isn't that community?

Is extremism in any pursuit a vice or virtue?

Do we believe that there is a solution for every problem?

In some nations why does religion have to go underground? Isn't that a travesty that must be cured?

What about research on human and animal subjects? What about witch doctors? What about medical ethics?

Can anything be done on Earth that is positive without a great deal of effort? Doesn't every positive thing accomplished create inspiration for others to carry on?

Do we disregard the simplest laws of nature? What is in us that allows us to continue on the path of environmental destruction? Why lay that burden on future generations? Why injure planet Earth with our disregard for its environment? Will we survive but not Earth? Is that a possibility?

Do we recognize our own limitations? Are they real or are they self-imposed negative restrictions?

Do victory and defeat really mean anything? When trial comes, how do we react? Does positive thinking really work?

Do we abuse the right of free speech and free press?

If we hear the phrase, "the balance of life," do we think that it refers to all aspects of life including spirituality? Why aren't we willing to leave our personal safety and comfort and plunge into life? Do we have faith in humanity?

Aren't we tired of all the surveys and analyses of human study, that become just statistics sitting on a shelf?

Aren't we part of the whole? So what about drugs, the grower, the pusher and the user? If we believe we're one, what does that say to us?

Do we wish we had a crystal ball to see into the future? Can we control the next moment?

Are we curious for the sake of curiosity? What intrigues us about the unknown? Is it to avoid the present?

Is this the time to ask why or why not? Or so what?

How and why do we endure sickness and other tribulations? What about holistic health centers?

Why waste life? What about abortion and euthanasia? Is the choice always ours?

Shouldn't we cling to hope and not get dragged into a cesspool of despair?

Is there any difference between verbal and physical abuse?

Have we, or the institutionalized church, tried to bury Jesus Christ?

Where is the good news? Are we only interested in sensationalism? Why do the good things in life get ignored and the evil things get coverage? Is it a ploy to sell the news by panic?

Is there such a thing as the power of prayer? If we pray, don't we need to believe? Aren't or shouldn't our daily actions be prayer in motion? When we think of what's wrong and what we can do about it, isn't it then when prayer begins? Doesn't prayer make us grow towards the light?

When we raise money for food and other help campaigns, how is it spent?

What is the deepest value we teach our children in the "formal" educational system? Isn't the educational system preparing our children to live in our society, our global society? Then shouldn't love be woven into the system?

Do we tend to take each other for granted? What about the homeless? What about the hungry?

Are we fed a daily dose of negativity because we are more interested in suffering than joy?

Why do we want others to give us our happiness? Doesn't our happiness stem from giving to others?

Is there really an ulterior motive to "New Age" thinking? If there is, what is it?

What is the "invisible energy" that scientists talk about? Is it the "glue" that keeps the planet together? Are we the "glue"?

Do we feel entrapped by our circumstances? Is it easier to blame circumstances rather than ourselves?

Do we run from our own existence?

Have we fractured our hope?

When we seek success, what part, in our search, does our attitude play? Does prosperity bring perils and responsibility?

Isn't it true that we have learned a great deal about our planet? But does our knowledge include the weave of God our Father?

Can the impatience of youth be fired up to create a better society?

Isn't it true that all communication with God our Father takes place through prayer? Doesn't prayer lift us out of despair and give us peace, hope and direction? Isn't life a prayer?

Do we take ourselves too seriously?

Aren't all of our adversities really opportunities?

How can we blame all the disasters that have affected us as a people on our leaders? What is our part? Have we been active or inactive?

Can we visualize peace into existence? Why not?

Isn't our purpose to become involved personally with Christ, so we can fulfill our roles in history, the history that's made everyday?

Aren't we all in the same predicament in life? Who has it easy? Doesn't each one of us carry our own cross? Who can weigh the burden that besets each one of us? In the end, aren't they all relative?

If we don't believe that it's possible to create a society inspired by God, how do we believe in the power of God our Father, the oneness of the human family, the divine within, the truth? Why not believe? Don't we have to believe?

Is the in-thing of the day, to be a channeler? Is it a diversion or is it growth to seek channelers?

If we are in need, should we simply ask in prayer? If our need is in concert with the will of God our Father, won't we receive it if we have faith? If we have faith, haven't we already received it?

Why not visualize the power of healing through Jesus Christ? Isn't everything with God possible?

Why is it so hard to accept change? Do we spend too much time looking backwards?

How important is it to preserve the integrity of the family unit? Isn't preservation of the family, preservation of our future?

Should we have to sell our morals in order to succeed in today's business world?

What criminal acts do we commit against the animal kingdom? What senseless slaughter is justified? Why not animal rights?

Do we really support each other? Or do we go along for the ride?

Isn't it true that in order to make a proper decision, we need to use the approach of indifference? Wouldn't that help us be objective and not go along with the crowd? Might it not give us the courage to break the chains of bondage? Will it help us stretch our imaginations to do more for society? Can we be indifferent to health versus sickness, prosperity versus poverty, honor versus dishonor? Will it help, if we know it is in tune with the living God?

Isn't it amazing when we observe people who are in very poor health but have a good attitude and outlook on life? What makes them behave that way? Could it be their personal relationship with God our Father?

Why is Jesus Christ pigeonholed into a religious category?

Have we noticed how some of the poorest of the poor have a deep contentment? Have they found the secret to life? The living God our Father within?

If millions upon millions are malnourished, why do we waste food? If one is hungry, aren't we all hungry?

Where has common sense gone?

WHEN we are poor in spirit, weak and oppressed, and we turn to God our Father in faith and hope, he will console us with his overwhelming love. When we are meek and rely on the inner strength of God to give us courage, he will grant us superpowers to combat injustice. When we are afflicted, we are afflicted in Christ who consoles, creating an inner sense of peace by opening our hearts to comfort others. When we hunger and thirst for justice, the living God feeds us with his spirit, which satisfies and strengthens us with hope and courage. When we are merciful to others, we are also merciful to ourselves, for we are one in the same. When we are pure in heart, the living God protects us from all forms of temptation that divert us from our destiny. When we are peacemakers, we are doing the will of Jesus Christ, who is one with the Father and we are one with him. When we suffer persecution for the sake of justice and reject bondage and slavery, we are healed by the living God, our Father, so that our persecution becomes our ticket home.

"Seek first the kingdom of God and his justice, and he will give us all those other things as well."
Luke 12:31

CHAPTER 15

To Create a World More Human and More Divine*

I believe we can change this world of ours into a world more human and more divine, and believe it or not, it's simple and exciting. Together, while keeping our diversity as a people, we are one in this challenging and ongoing adventure. This lifelong journey is not centered around the building of nursing homes, schools, or hospitals, nor is it a fundraiser for any particular organization or religious denomination. It is centered around all of us, as individuals, and it's based on love. There are no special classes or books needed; the only requirement is our love and the power of Jesus Christ that comes with it by simply living life to the fullest and loving one another.

---

*©Copyright 1983 by Anthony G. Bottagaro. All rights reserved. This message, as referenced in the introduction, is reprinted here in its entirety.

Before I continue, I thought it would be appropriate to make a statement on the focus of this mission and where I stand in my relationship to Christ and his message as it relates to the world today. First, I have been asked by others to describe and explain the focus of creating a world more human and more divine in greater detail, or in other words, what's really the bottom line. The fact is there is only one purpose or focus and that's simply to create a society inspired by God through love. Second, I'm just an ordinary person and I have no secrets or hidden motives in the role I play in this endeavor. I know that God has blessed me with a wonderful wife, five great children, and a life that's full; and I choose of my own free will and out of love to serve Him to the best of my abilities. I wish for no money or rewards in this service, and by working in the business sector I'll provide my own resources to spread the word of God. What I'm to say I believe, for I speak not from textbooks or theological courses, but from the heart, and from my own experiences and those of others. I believe the word of God and love Him, and my faith in Jesus Christ is irrevocable. I have no doubts, no reservations, no hesitations in my belief in Him, the living Christ. Jesus is first in my life, and without His hand on me, I am absolutely nothing and I thank Him for giving me life.

All that I do is for God with the accolades going one way, to Him. In whatever I do, my goal is simply to be His servant in conveying the message of Christ which is rooted in love. I accept Christ as the way, the truth, and the life. However, I support, acknowledge, and encourage the spiritual truths found among all people because we all share a common destiny, unity in God.

I believe in the message of Christ with its foundation of love being the conduit in which God works, and how He works in each of our lives is found in our own personal relationship with Him. I believe in the power of God, and not of man; and only through God doing the conversion of mind toward love with the cooperation of man, can we achieve a world more human and more divine. The only thing I can do is speak His truth and then rely on Him. The sun of God shines, and the rain of God falls on all people. He doesn't have any favorites nor is there any exclusivity with Him. He works in the freedom of personhood, and I won't judge or undercut or ridicule the faith of any person; that's not my concern. Where that person is in his or her relationship to God is only between that person and God. What's critical in today's society is that the dignity of all people be preserved. We have to respect where a person is at his or her time in life. How can we accept God as our Father from whom we all come and then discriminate against others and look upon our personhood differently and not acknowledge the equality of all people?

My belief is in the divinity and doctrine of Christ, and if I can in my small way spread His word of love, to me that's enough, for I trust and know my God, and I believe in His power and His promises to us and in His ability to fulfill them. I believe that when all people of all nations accept and adopt the simple message of

Christ, which can be summed up in one word, "Love," then and only then can this earth have the total joy and peace that He promised.

I have been asked if I've originated any new concepts or message toward the goal of creating a world more human and more divine. That's exactly what I have not done. The problem in my opinion is that we have complicated the message of Christ and have tried every now and then to camouflage it, when in fact it's simple enough for all people, not only to understand, but to live. Because we are all one in God and children of God, there's that natural commonality of sisterhood and brotherhood among all of us. There's no need for any dividing lines. We, and not God, have set up all the rules, regulations, structures, nations, and boundaries. There is no mountain, ocean, or any natural boundary that separates us as a people. There is no difference between people except what we choose to call different: the difference of color, friends, or enemies, relatives or strangers, nationalities, and so on. Nor is there any civil law that divides us as a people except the laws and boundaries that we have established within our hearts.

All of us, we are the key, we are all responsible for the happenings on this earth. We are the people, from poor to rich, with our individual gifts, personalities, qualities, and temperaments, we are the church, all of us, together, and when we stand before God, we stand as one, there are no distinctions.

Cardinal Suenens says: "Prudence is everywhere, courage is nowhere, and soon we shall all die of wisdom." In my opinion, we all need to accept the call to courage and to trust God in our use of prudence.

There was a time when Jesus was asked this question: "Which is the greatest commandment of the Law?" He replied, "You must love the Lord your God with all your heart, soul, mind, and strength. The second is this: You must love your neighbor as yourself. There is no commandment greater, and on these the whole law is based." Then, at the Last Supper He said: "This is my commandment, love one another as I have loved you. A man can have no greater love than to lay down his life for his friends." When we tie these three commandments together, it sums up in real simple terms what God expects of us and what Jesus Christ did for us; and therein lies the basis of the Gospel and our guide to life. If we can implant these thoughts in our minds, life will take on new meaning and will be uncomplicated because Jesus Christ did not want the word of God complicated. In fact, he made it simple enough to be revealing to little children. We need to accept His word with the simplicity and the trust of a child-like heart.

However, by using worldly intellect and parameters, do we complicate the simple message of Jesus Christ?

Why are we sometimes deaf, dumb, and blind when we search for God in this world of ours? What was said thousands of years ago is applicable today. When the Holy Spirit spoke, he told our ancestors through the prophet Isaiah: "Go to this nation and say, you will hear and hear again, but not understand, see and see again but not perceive. For the heart of this nation has grown coarse, their ears are dull of hearing and they have shut their eyes, for fear they should see with their eyes, hear with their ears, understand with their heart, and be converted and healed by me."

What's interesting is that man is always on some type of quest, crusade, or campaign as he or she searches for God and tries to make this world more liveable. We have gone the way of the peace march, the walk for desegregation, we have tried sit-ins, protests, civil disobedience and we have even resorted to wars or whatever the "in" thing of the day happens to have been. You name it, man has tried it, we have tried it all. And what has it gained us? We see temporary relief in some cases, total failure in others, and hollow victories in still others.

Doesn't it seem odd that even though our quality of life has improved greatly in most of the world, that the anxieties, fears, mistrust, and threats have grown with it? "It" is the so-called quality of life. The time is ripe to start now and put the past behind us, as our concern should be for the present, for that's the only moment we have control over. The thing that I find most interesting is that because love is inbred and natural to us, people can easily relate to what love provides; and they're really searching for a way to express it and recognize it in others. It seems like each one is waiting for the other person to start the deep bond of friendship and then together to reach out and strengthen that friendship among all people. The level of trust and understanding we have with one another can be cultivated; for if love is to grow, trust and understanding have to grow with it, and until we can see ourselves and place ourselves in each other's position and viewpoint, we will never develop a deep bond of understanding. The old adage "bear one another's burdens and joys and fulfill the law of Christ" is a truism.

What happens to us? Do we get our priorities turned around as we become involved in this world of ours, or do we get confused with all the slogans, movements, and every conceivable structure known to mankind? And to what and to whom do we relate, the structure or the simple command of Jesus Christ to serve and love God and one another?

Why do we thrive on competition? I'm not referring to individual creativity and competition in the world of sports and business. No, I am referring to the small thinking and pettiness of one-upsmanship in our everyday encounters. At times it seems that without conflict and competition among people in one form or another, we would be lost. What is it that drives us in that direction? Don't we think we're deserving of peace and love and self-respect and all those things that seem like pie in the sky? If creating a world more human and more divine is pie in the sky, then we might as well pack up our bags and go to the nearest hole and wait until we die into nothingness.

The cross of Christ is the sign of God's universal love. We as a people in our relationship with God the Father and in our relationship with each other are so intertwined and so dependent on each other that, as Holy Scripture says, "Whoever who does not love, does not know God."

We as a people are always rallying around somebody or something. What we need to do is to rally around Christ rather than around some rational philosophy based on the principles of this world. Do we worry and wait for somebody to inspire us and tell us what to do to create a better world? Well, we don't have to worry or wait if we just ask God's blessing and pray for His grace. We can put on Christ, and as we become more like Christ, nobody will have to tell us what to do, we will all know what to do. For how can we be like Christ and not know what to do? Then, our foundations will be as solid as a rock and with total clarity, we'll be able to re-evaluate our involvement with the structures of this world as we create a society inspired by God.

This earth of ours is our current home, and God has entrusted us with it. If we recall, Christ did not ask for us to be removed from the world. He said, "Father, as you sent me into the world, I have sent them into the world." Jesus Christ is sending us into the world to make it more human and more divine.

His state was divine, yet He did not cling to His equality with God but He emptied Himself to assume the condition of a servant. Love our God, as He loves us, unconditionally, and serve and love our neighbor. However, we can't love our neighbor until we love ourselves, and this is the key to our mission. The role we fill here on earth, which may seem insignificant to us, is of great importance to God. It doesn't matter how little or how great our role may seem; what's important is how well we play it. A good self-image will create within us a Christ-like foundation upon which to build our lives, with love as our cornerstone.

Instead of pointing out all the things that are wrong with church, society, politics, the world in general, why don't we point to the way that Christ instructed us, to love and serve one another? We can't be concerned with what the next person is doing, or what the politicians or religious are doing, and so on, until we concern ourselves with what and who we are. If we begin with ourselves first, and as we change and put on Christ, then the love and power that flows from within will inspire the people around us, and that's one sure way we can build unity among people. Perseverance is the key; there's no need to give up on ourselves or get discouraged, whether in criticism, or apathy as we move constantly toward the goal of love.

If all of us who are involved in this pursuit blank from our minds the pride or individualism that stems from trying to build little domains, then with total harmony the words should and will turn into deeds. As old hat as it may sound, integrity and truth, especially with ourselves, will free us from a singleness to unity. I really don't believe there's a single person out there who, in the quiet of his or her soul, doesn't want a world more human and more divine. I refuse to believe that we can't change this world. Who in the world can argue with the loving message of Christ?

As we become more like Christ, a new awareness takes hold and we longer have to conform to worldly standards and values with our new Christ-like mind. We then can change the standards and values of the world. God, through Christ, is calling all people to Himself and enlisting them in this ongoing and love-inspired adventure. He is always there, ready to guide us on this credible journey with the same enthusiasm that we have in pursuing it, His children doing His work on earth.

I ask you, if God is for us, who is against us? We have got to believe, believe in ourselves, believe in all people, no exceptions, believe that the power of Christ can transform people who will in turn radiate this earth of ours with love. To do our thing, whatever that is, without love in our hearts is likened to a race where the thrill of victory and agony of defeat is the same, and the short lived excitement is the anticipation that leads up to the race, the race itself, and when it's over, nothing.

Love is in us and is always straining to be released. The power of love based on Christ is a force so powerful that it's incomprehensible. We all know it, and all we have to do is to accept it and bring it to our conscious mind. When we can acknowledge and respect ourselves as to where we are in life and acknowledge the spiritual truths of all people and where they are in life, then we will be able to show our inner strength and faith in ourselves and God.

Enthusiasm, generosity, and love, those are the things that ignite us in Christianity. We are not a religion of despair, but of hope. We need to accept our human responsibility out of love and not fear.

So, we may or may not choose to print signs or join activist groups, or have long mental dissertations to arrive at some exotic plan of action, for activity without love has no permanent impact on life; nor do we have to wait until Sunday or some other day. Today is the day, why wait, we can begin now, and it's simple and exciting. All we have to do is put on Christ, live life to the fullest and love one another.

A World More Human and More Divine

Lip service takes us just so far. It's not just a matter of practicing what we preach, but goes beyond that in our normal everyday encounters, and if we don't follow through on our promises to one another and commitments to one another, how can we build the trust relationship that's needed to instill total love in our lives? People like to get involved when they feel they can benefit; however, whether or not we interact with one another, each of us affects the other person's life; that's a plain and simple fact. There's a natural impulse and mutual advantage to helping one another, for we're all one in God. The common denominator is not religion, but it's God, who is love, and God is a 24 hour commitment every day of our lives. Religion is a means, and God is an end.

Love is contagious and so is happiness. Our love and the love and power of Christ is a force so strong that with that combination there's nothing on this earth that couldn't be changed for the better. Saint Paul hit the nail on the head, and it's written down and recorded in history for all to read and understand. It can be found in 1 Corinthians, Chapter 13, Verses 1-13, and I believe it's the key in finding the answers to our problems. In essence, he said: "If I have all the eloquence of men or the gift of prophecy and know everything, and if I have faith to move mountains and give away all I possess but I am without love, then I am nothing at all." He concluded with: "There are three things that last: faith, hope, and love, and the greatest of these is love because God is love." True love requires sacrifice, for the fact is that true love considers the other person first, love endures all.

So we can read all the books in the world from the motivational type to spiritual writings, or go to the finest universities, or be a great tradesman, salesman, doctor, or whatever our earthly vocation happens to be, but greatness without love is nothing, for without love we have no foundation. Whatever we create and establish for society, if it was created without love, we have accomplished nothing; for without love, it just can't last.

It takes courage and truth for all those involved in service to face people and say, "We need you as a person of God with love and your individual talents in assisting each other," period; no more need be said. I believe if people are approached with that attitude, an attitude of love and trust, the response will be overwhelming in support, and the return will be a thousandfold. If we give money to benefit hospitals, schools, and other institutions, or give of our talent, but if it's devoid of love, it simply has a zero effect on life. We, as individuals, have great human resources. When we share those resources in whatever we are and whatever we do, with one another, out of love, then the residual effect we have on society will be lasting and will multiply itself as the earth gets tugged toward the Kingdom of God.

Our mission will not be accomplished until all men and women rid themselves of hate, built-up prejudices, pride, greed, and blindness to the injustices that are created on earth. Isn't it about time that all the words and pledges of all institutions and structures have a common goal toward creating a world more human and more divine? Or will once again the words of the prophet Isaiah ring true as he says, "You will hear and hear again but not understand, see and see again but not perceive."

Instead of competition and fragmentation, we need to encourage cooperation among the various denominations and service organizations by simply acknowledging to all people that the underlying purpose is to spread the Kingdom of God. The message of Christ has always been love, and it hasn't changed; although we may use different methods and take different roads to accomplish our goals, they all lead to the kingdom of the one God: a Kingdom that's universal, a Kingdom of truth and life, a Kingdom of justice, love and peace.

When we as a people, one by one, put on Christ and live and love one another, then the answers to the problems that beset this world of ours will become apparent through the process of love; and therein lies the basis for peace and the renewal of family, the answer to injustice, drug addiction and abuse, and therein lies the basis and answer to solve our hunger and poverty problems that exist in this world, and so on. The solutions are there. With faith we can do it, as our minds and hearts accept the love of God, and then planted in love and built on love we become more like Christ, and we will know what to do, as the words turn into deeds enabling us to live life to the fullest as we love one another.

We have to be optimistic in our approach to creating a world more human and more divine, and we have great company in this adventure as Jesus Christ is the eternal optimist. Did He Himself not leave behind a small group of ordinary men to carry on His word?

Jesus Christ is counting on us, we, His people, to act on His word by simply living life to the fullest and loving one another.

This is my way; and I look forward to meeting you on the roadway of love. So as we participate in our respective houses of worship and service organizations, and as we relate and interact with one another in our jobs, homes and everyday encounters with and through love, we create a world more human and more divine.

I ask you, is there any greater challenge or adventure for a life more natural and more exciting?

"WITH LOVE . . . PASS IT ON"

CHAPTER 16
Together We Can

It has been said that I do not advocate movements.
It has been said that I do not advocate demonstrations.
It has been said that I do not advocate legal action.
It has been said that I do not advocate political action.
It has been said that I do not advocate simple protest.
It has been said that I do not advocate civil disobedience.

One more time, for the record, what I do advocate is love. The simple power of love. However, it is beyond my wildest imagination how one could love and not act when he or she thought it appropriate. I believe the time has come to eliminate all the what if's, the why's and the why not's. I refuse to believe we cannot change this world of ours through the subtle power of love.

The following are the fourteen planks that make up the platform for *REVOLUTION: A CHALLENGE OF LOVE*:

We can rise up and tear from our eyes the veil that separates us by color, race, sex, language, religion and nationality. Then we can acknowledge to each other that we are a united people who are ready and prepared to do battle for revolution.
Together we can.

We can rise up, though we are poor in spirit, to help others, for we know we are full of life and love. We can heed the cry from our thirsty, hungry, homeless and poverty-stricken brothers and sisters and wipe away the tears from the lonely. Let us radiate the world with our compassion and forgiveness for each other.
Together we can.

We can rise up and show the leadership of our governments and religions that we are not apathetic, complacent or unaware, but concerned people who do not want counterfeit freedom, but true freedom. We can go to the aid of those seeking asylum and those in exile, so they can be free. We can make our voices and actions heard and felt, so we can free hostages, find the missing and support the refugees. Let us seek not "worldly" comfort or security, revenge or popularity, but fundamental freedoms and justice for all people.
Together we can.

We can rise up and shatter the illusion of exaggeration caused by the lie. We can crack the seams of secrecy, bitterness and malice to let the light shine in. We can put to sleep pride, self-pity, intolerance and anger so we can reveal our true selves. Let us awaken our apathy to challenge the system with love, so we can serve each other.
Together we can.

We can rise up and shed the tar of weakness and/or guilt to reveal our strength, cloaked in gentleness and kindness, and spread it throughout the planet. We can lift ourselves above our sorrow and move forward with joy in sacrifice for others. Let us pardon those who have injured us, thereby healing all.
Together we can.

We can rise up as peacemakers, not warmakers disguised as doves, and gain victory over the threat of war and war itself once and for all. Let us use our understanding, trustfulness and patience in society as stepping stones to peace. We can rip ruthlessness, repression and rejection out of the system and plant love. Let us use the method of non-violence against any form of violence and crumble it to pieces.
Together we can.

We can rise up and demand basic human rights for those who are denied jobs, fair wages and working conditions, peaceful assembly and freedom of speech and belief. We can release our fear and break wide open the conspiracy of silence that inflicts internal and external harm to all people. Let us show friend and foe alike that we are not tired or oppressed, but are full of enthusiasm and energy and will not wear down when it comes to upholding the birthrights of all people.
Together we can.

We can rise up, match our words with our deeds, and expose and rout out those who use exploitation and manipulation as their weapon. We can sink all hostility, slaughter, savagery, arrogance and corruption into the bottom of the sea. Let us overpower with love those who employ arbitrary arrest and inflict torture as their method to rule.
Together we can.

We can rise up with courage and use our faith to destroy doubt. We can melt away hardness of heart and hypocrisy with a fusion of the heart and mind. With love, we can stamp out fanaticism, cynicism, aggression and tyranny wherever it exists. Let us lock out, from our hearts, paranoia, conceit, jealousy and greed so we can leave room for faith, hope and love.
Together we can.

We can rise up and renew our families with a bond of love so strong that nothing will crack or break it. We can help those in need of housing and employment with our resources. We can crush and conquer, without compromise, drug suppliers, drug addiction and drug abuse. Only we can eliminate crime from our streets and our corporate board-rooms. Let us diffuse our communities of vengeance, deceit, treachery and antagonism.
Together we can.

We can rise up and use our technical knowledge and healing power of the heart to eradicate disease and provide health care for those in need. We can save our planet from the deadly fate of pollution by cleaning up our environment. We can encourage an educational system that teaches love and unity and gives hope to our children. Let us use our gifts of hope and enlightenment to spread our light and break the darkness. With our light, we can answer the questions of abortion and euthanasia.
Together we can.

We can rise up, though persecuted, to abolish forever any form of bondage and slavery and to reinstate the dignity of all people. We can fight and defeat those who inflict cruel, degrading and inhumane treatment or punishment on others. Though we may mourn, let us use our inbred joy to lift the hearts of the depressed.
Together we can.

We can rise up and let the leaders of our governments and religions know that we are not chasing dreams of fantasy, but seeking systems that exist for the benefit and support of all people. Let it be known to all, especially the establishment, both religious and secular, that in our revolution we will not succumb to any wrong or any outrage, whether in thought or action, committed against any person, anywhere, for we are one.
Together we can.

We can rise up, each of us, and accept our responsibility to acknowledge and accept the gift of life, light and truth. We can rise up and let the universe know that our only weapon is love in the battle for revolution, and nothing has been or ever will be manufactured that can defeat love.
Together we can.

The revolution has begun. The battle will continue to rage. We cannot forget anyone in the battle for revolution. Let us dare each other, again and again, to join the ranks of the "invisible" army of people, those who fight daily, the fight of faith, against the powers of darkness, who perpetuate injustice. The decision is ours. Victory is ours. Immortality and destiny are ours. What will history write about this generation? Will it say that we were so fragile and afraid that we would crack and break, that we sat back and did nothing? Or will it say that we were willing to risk our reputations, if necessary, our very lives for each other, and fight in the battle for REVOLUTION? How long will the battle last? Who knows? But we do know that the efforts of this generation will set the pace and give hope for those who follow. Let us together show them our courage.

Let us not underestimate our adversary, for it is cunning and flaunts the power of the world. However, we can bring it to its knees with love and with our ability to take whatever consequences come our way and still love. We are naive if we think we can wage this battle without sacrifice. Yet sacrifice is the very thing that will lead us to victory, our destiny. Victory will come through sacrifice. We are revolutionaries through the love of the cross. We have to be willing to pay any price for victory. We cannot win the battle with defense alone. We must thrust the offensive power of love into all aspects of life.

All of the "**together we can's**" need to be wrapped in a blanket of love, as love is the one enduring solution to all of our problems. Out of love, let us, together, crush and shatter the mountain of injustice to a pile of dust. Let those who are timid find strength in each other, for we need everyone. You can make a difference. No one is immune from evil as long as it exists, for if it attacks others, it has indeed attacked us. That is an absolute fact. So join in the fight right now. Let us together, out of love, continue to pound away and disintegrate the edifice of evil that exists throughout the mountain of injustice. Let us pound and pound away, until we give it its final death blow. Final victory is imminent and will be ours. A victory inspired through love for the honor and glory of the living God our Father.

I ask, challenge, dare and call each one of you to join me in the following revolutionary actions:

• Please acknowledge the twelve DECLARATIONS of REVOLUTION by signing on page 13.

• Let us continue to make known the demands of the declarations of revolution to everyone who affects our lives, especially our leaders, so we and they can live out the declarations through love.

• Choose as your special focus any one or more of the 14 planks that comprise the revolution platform. Then, personally, through love, take responsibility, and act in any non-violent action to help fulfill the vision of *REVOLUTION: A CHALLENGE OF LOVE*.

• Beginning January 7, 1990, and continuing on the first Sunday of every January thereafter, celebrate the world-wide "**Together We Can**" breakfast. This breakfast is intended to be open to everyone, anywhere in the world, you choose the place. In order for this event to be effective and significant, it will take an organized plan of action on your part, as each breakfast is independent of the other, yet through the spirit they are all fused together as one. At the breakfast we can recommit and recruit others to the challenge of love and vision of revolution. We then can reconfirm that "**together we can**," through love, make a difference.

We are spirit, and we live and will never taste death. We are four and a half billion people on Earth. We are power. We are truth. We are free.

I look forward to hearing your voices and seeing your actions as a united people in the battle for

REVOLUTION: A CHALLENGE OF LOVE. I know we shall meet on the roadway. Let us remember the battle cry, **"together we can"** . . . **and together we will.**

The journey continues . . .

ABOUT THE AUTHOR

Anthony G. Bottagaro, a seasoned executive, is author of the highly acclaimed book TO CREATE A WORLD MORE HUMAN AND DIVINE. In 1984, he produced and narrated a documentary film of the same title. The film was premiered at the United Nations, and he was awarded two prestigious Angel Awards for Excellence in Media for the book and film.

Bottagaro has taken his film and its message to such diverse places as the University of Peace in Costa Rica, the White House, the State Department, the Pentagon, the World Conference of Religion and Peace, the World Council of Churches and a number of Geneva-based international peace organizations.

In 1987, he personally presented a copy of the book and film to Pope John Paul II at the Vatican.

Bottagaro and his wife, Cathy, have five children, and reside in Boulder, Colorado.

ORDER INFORMATION

Two ways to order
REVOLUTION: A CHALLENGE OF LOVE
The book that will change your life forever!

— From your local bookstore

— Direct from the publisher:
Interloc Publishing Inc.
P.O. Box 79
Boulder, Colorado 80306
(303) 440-9565

$14.95 plus $2.00 postage and handling.
Colorado residents please add 3.6% state sales tax
Boulder residents please add 6.13% sales tax

* * * * *

Lectures, Seminars and Workshops

For information concerning lectures, seminars, and workshops, contact Interloc Seminars, P.O. Box 79, Boulder, Colorado 80306 or call (303) 440-9565

NOTES

NOTES

NOTES

NOTES

NOTES

NOTES

NOTES

NOTES

NOTES

NOTES